Nana's Shoes

A Story of a Family's Faith, Hope, and Courage in a Time of Ethnic Cleansing

by

Aisa Softic

For : Ms. Bonarrigo

From: Suada

ISBN 9780996294911

Cover design by Ms. Feiruz Bakthir

Dear Donna,

Was my Plesure working with you and I will miss you!
As a child, I grow up in a country where there was a lot separation among children, but growing up a person get used to it becomes normal.
My languge teacher was a big racist and I was a 5th grader didn't understand that, but I did later as an adult.
I sufferd so mutch in that class that I started to hate reading and books and writing, becouse what ever I did was not enoug or not good at all even if it was same as some other kids my was not good becouse I was muslim.
& When you offerd me position as Gibrarian I was scared at first.
I thought oh no what I feard all my life now I have to face it. →

May 2021

Dear Donna,

... like my pressure working with you and I will miss you!

As a child, I grew up in a country where there was a lot of separation among children, but growing up a person get used to it because its normal.

My language teacher was a big racist and I was a 5th grader didn't understand that, but I did later as an adult.

I suffered so much in that class. I started to hate reading and books and writing, because what ever I did was not enough or not good at all even it it was not good because I was muslim. some as some other kids my

When you offered me position as Librarian I was scared at first. I thought oh no what I stood all my life now I have to face it I

But now I am happy that you did it because it gave me renewed Desire to read and ~~lot~~ love for the Books.

As you can see I am giveing you a book that is the true story of an friend of mine who was older when she went through

In the name of God, the Beneficent, the Merciful

the war and I was 14 years old. But by Gods will we meat here in Boston and becom friends.

This Book showes a life of many people during the war for some worse and some litlu better. I am glad I had opporteirnts to escape the war and come here where I would be fair treatu

Thank you for giving me the opportunity to be what I can be and not what I have to.

Love   Suada   Mansouri

A Map[1]

---

[1] Map from www.mappery.com

Editor's Preface: An Odyssey

By John Overbeck

There are books that ought to be read.

Nana's Shoes, a memoir by Aisa Softic, is not one of those books.

Nana's Shoes is a book that **must** be read.

Aisa, a Bosnian Muslim, has written an odyssey, a story that takes its readers through a range of challenges that pit the human spirit against the odds and provide lessons in courage for us all.

The story of Aisa and her family is a Bosnian and a Muslim story, but it is above all else a human story.

Born in 1950 to a hard-working farm family that owned its own land but wrested only subsistence from it, Aisa was destined to half an education and a life of hard work, little financial gain, and the obscurity of the poor.

But God decreed otherwise, and gave to Aisa gifts that cannot be purchased with money: the gifts of faith, an abundance of family love and support, intelligence, courage, and an indomitable spirit.

Aisa earned her education and became a teacher and a high school principal. And, when Yugoslavia (which included Bosnia) broke up and descended into violence and the ethnic cleansing of Muslims, she held tight to her family at the risk of her own life and saw all of her family members – her husband, their daughter and son, and herself – safely to the United States to begin life anew.

Nana's Shoes is about a brave woman and her family. At the same time it is a story of how, when the human spirit rises up and speaks courage to violence, courage wins out.

A book that **must** be read.

Editor's Preface

By: Azra Husejnovic

Many memoirs and stories about war frequently come from a male perspective. Aisa's story is refreshing in that it shows what living and surviving through a brutal war is like as a woman and a working mother. Aisa's faith in God and Islam is inspiring, as she describes what it is like to grow up poor struggling to finish her education, sending her sixteen-year old daughter to America for a better future, and saving her family from multiple dangers throughout the war. Aisa faced too many close calls with soldiers threatening her life, her family's life, her home, and any hope of a future in her home country. Her faith in God during each of those struggles is what guides her through and ultimately to a better ending. She is not only the hero of this survivor story, but also a role model to all strong, independent, and faithful women today.

Growing up as a refugee myself in war-torn Sarajevo, Bosnia myself, Aisa's story hits home on multiple levels. She perfectly captures the emotions that any refugee faces; the shock, the cold never ending fear, the paralyzing effects of seeing blood spattered on the streets, the blatant discrimination against one group of people, the struggles to provide food and shelter for your family, the heart-racing moments looking over your shoulder and hearing the stories of other women being rapped, the never ending longing for one day that this will all end...I know that other survivors of the Bosnian genocide as well as the wars going on today such as in Palestine and Syria can relate to these struggles. I hope we can all learn from Aisa and her admirable persistence in getting her family to a safer place, and ultimately to be grateful for all that God has given each and every one of you. And most of all, I hope that by telling this story we will learn from our past and never let this happen again.

Author's Preface

Humans need to use words to communicate, and keep their weapons quiet. War is the worst disaster humans can face. It is worse than earthquakes, tornadoes, hurricanes, and tsunamis because people purposely harm other people, creating an army of mourners, refugees, disabled persons, and raped women.

My thirteen-year-old son, eighty-seven-year-old mother-in-law, and I stayed in our home in Bosnia to witness the war's destruction, but at the same time, we viewed God's miracles. My only weapons were my prayers. I never prayed more seriously—crying out and asking for God's protection—as I did during the war. Every night could have been my last. God heard our prayers, protected us when we were very close to death, and sent good people to help us survive—so I offer Him my undying gratitude.

Nana's Shoes is the story of my family's journey as one among many journeys of my beloved Bosnian people. I want to thank all those who loved our country of Bosnia more than their lives. I want to encourage people to work toward ending all wars and to work together to create peace on this earth.

All of the events in this book are true stories I received permission to use some people's real names, but some names have been changed to protect people from negative associations.

My dream of writing a book became reality with help of many people: my dear husband Husein Softic, our daughter Aida Zvekic and her husband Suvad, our son Samir Softic and his wife Norah, and our dear grandchildren—Ammar and Mensur Zvekic and Arif and Laila Softic. Ms. Azra Husejnovic, Mr. John Overback, Ms. Feiruz Bakhtim, Ms. Sanja Bilic, Mr. Brian Eastman, Mrs. Phyllis Schomaker, Ms. Karen Heaster, Mrs. Janice Cubbison, Mr. Roger Argalas, Mrs. Angelina Joseph, Mrs. Jane Holt, Mrs. Dianne Sunderman, Mrs. Joy Dickinson, Mrs. Barbara Prat, Mrs. Tammy Froehle, Mrs. Debbie Redmon, Mrs. Diane Ritter, Mrs. Molie Shamma, Mrs. Freda Shamma, Mrs. Marce Epstein, cousins, friends, and colleagues—too many to mention—you know who you are and I thank you.

My name is Aisa Softic and these are my stories.

Table of Contents

You were born to make manifest the Glory of God that is within you. It is not just in some of us; it's in everyone. And, as you let your own light shine, you unconsciously give other people permission to do the same.

—Nelson Mandela

Prologue—The Night in the Cornfield

Humans transgress all limits when they feel that there is no one above them.

In the beginning of July1993, the news of our neighbor Mirsad Kovacevic's death spread like wild fire, consuming all joy of life and suffocating the entire the village of Dubrave in grief. I wanted to scream at the top of my lungs to shake and rattle all who were bent on injustice.

I walked through the house with my heart as hard as a sunbaked field in July. Suddenly, several knocks on my window redirected my thoughts and sorrow. My neighbor Mina was motioning me to come outside. When I approached her she whispered, "Today is our Judgment Day." She wiped the sweat from her forehead and looked around. "One of the Serb soldiers has been wounded in battle today. If he dies tonight, the Serbs are going to kill all of us."

My heart skipped a beat, and I asked, "What should we do?"

"Run and hide in the cornfield. We cannot wait at home for our murderers to come."

A chill gripped me. Samir, my fourteen-year-old son, had not yet returned from my sister's home in Dubrave, and my mother-in-law could not walk as far as the cornfield.

"Wait a minute!" I raised my hand. "Wait! I must see to my son and Nana."

I ran to the garage, grabbed my bicycle, and pedaled as fast as I could toward Dubrave.

Dear God, protect my son and guide him safely home, I prayed. *Please protect him, protect him, and protect him*, I repeated with each push of the bicycle pedals. After about fifteen minutes of riding I noticed Samir and the invisible chains that had bound so tightly around me fell away.

"What happened, Mother?" He inquired, staring wide-eyed at me. "Where are you going?"

"I came to find you," I explained with a sigh, placing Samir's heavy milk containers on my bicycle and quietly thanking God that my son was safe. When I told him the news about Mirsad, the muscles of his face stiffened and fear filled his innocent, youthful eyes. War robs children of their sense of security.

When we entered our neighborhood, Samir frightened as a rabbit, looked around and whispered, "Mother, hurry up. Hurry up. It looks like all our neighbors have left their houses already."

"You must go with Mina's family." I looked at his eyes. "I'll join you in a little bit."

"Mother, please go with us," he whispered.

"Come out with the child immediately!" I recognized the strong voice of old Mehmed, Mina's father.

I signaled for Samir to go and opened the window. "What can I do with Nana? I must…"

"You must leave Nana," pleaded Mehmed. "You cannot sacrifice your life and the life of your child."

I said my evening prayer, lit a candle, and sat on the sofa close to Nana. Her shoes were delicately tied in her scarf. I looked at Nana, looked at the shoes and thought, *Can I ask Nana to put the shoes on and carry her on my back to the cornfield? Could I push her in a wheelbarrow? How could we cross the ditch? Nana could fall and break some of her bones. I need to leave Nana and the shoes where they are.* I pulled the door closed behind me. *Dear God, protect us. We are powerless.*

The coming night had begun to wrap itself around our small world and our great fears.

"Hurry up!" Mina whispered from her garden gate.

"I will stay here in my garden tonight," I confided, almost in tears. "I have to come back to check on Nana. I cannot leave her alone."

"I'm angry now," Mina moved closer to me. "Look, she has seven children. Two of her sons have been abroad for years. Why didn't they take her with them? It isn't fair."

"All of life is a test. Helping others brings blessings upon us," I replied. "Nana has lived with us for twenty years. She is the mother of my husband. She helped raise my children. I must protect her. But how can I do it?" I spoke hopelessly through my tears.

As though to make my decision for me, Mina grabbed my hand and yanked me forward. We hurried through our gardens as the last of the evening's golden light disappeared below the western horizon. Darkness and fear, its twin companion, walked with us as we moved quietly toward the deep ditch that separated us from the cornfield where we would lie in hiding through the night. I glanced back at the homes we had left, homes, which, in the ambient gloom of the night, had a look of sadness about them. Only one of them had a sign of life — one window where the flame of the candle I had lit sent forth its ray of hope. One small dancing light accompanied Nana as she sat in the house infirm and alone.

Oh, my dear Nana, forgive me tonight, I apologized from the bottom of my heart. *I couldn't take you with me, but my heart is aching at having to leave you. I couldn't even tell you that I left. How are you going to spend the night alone? You were afraid to sleep by yourself in your own room. Tonight you are alone not only in your room and in our house, but also in the entire neighborhood. Please forgive me. O merciful God, protect Nana tonight.*

"Aisa, hurry up," Mina whispered from the other side of the ditch.

I closed my fists, ran down the ditch, jumped over the narrow stream, grabbed some sturdy plants, and pulled myself up the bank. Mina grabbed my hand and helped me to the top. In front of us was a field with dark green corn stalks moving gently like waves on the Adriatic Sea. We reached Mina's family and Samir, sitting on blankets close to one another. I squatted next to my son and brushed his curly hair with my fingers.

"I hope we are safe here," whispered Nijaz, Mina's husband. "Our crazy Serb neighbors cannot cross the ditch in their cars to find us."

"This is ridiculous," Mina declared, raising her voice a little bit and turning toward her husband. "You can do what you want, but I'm going to get the documents I need and leave this hell with my children as soon as possible. I don't feel safe in this field. I want to be in a home or shelter far from bullets!"

Suddenly a warm wind brought with it a burning smell. A huge fire in the direction of our houses almost blinded me. I jumped. "Fire! My house is burning! Nana is there! Help! Help!" I screamed, running through the field.

"That isn't your house! My barn is burning! My poor cows!" Mehmed wrung his hands.

"You are both crazy tonight," Mina determined, standing in front of us. "The fire is far from our homes." She put one hand on her hip, and the other pointed in the direction of the fire. My eyes followed Mina's hand as it confirmed our error, but even so a cold

4

sweat covered me and I began to shake. I grabbed Mina's cotton bed sheet and wrapped myself in it. Mehmed was whispering prayers.

A deep, frightening darkness and moist chill spread through the field. I heard rifle fire in the distance and the gunshots sounded as though they were getting closer. The cries of children echoed in the cornfield. I stood up and paced a few steps. All of a sudden the voices of several men and human footsteps from nearby paralyzed my breath and stiffened my muscles. It looked like they were only a few meters from us. Instinctively I cowered behind a row of corn. Mehmed placed the white sheets under an empty basket and touched a finger to his lips for silence. We stayed still, with only our eyes moving, darting around in the darkness. As the voices became louder, drums sounds in my ears played faster. I closed my burning eyes, frightened at the thought of what I would see when I opened them. Breathing slowly through parted lips, I felt like a speck of dirt in the huge cornfield, unwilling to accept all of our tragedies but too weak to take control of our destinies.

Are they going to slaughter us? I asked myself without moving my lips. *Oh, no the children! Dear God, protect our children, all children, and protect all of us tonight. Make us invisible to our enemies.*

Then as quickly as they had come, the voices and sounds vanished, and I could breathe again. The children, exhausted from the tension, finally nodded off to sleep. I thanked God. My heart softened, and I found a little bit of peace. Eventually I fell asleep.

Roosters spread their songs through the entire field. The dawn's calm light appeared from the darkness. Mina and I woke the children, and we all slowly walked home. I found Nana sitting on her sofa, moving gently from side to side. Samir lay down close to her, curling his knees to his elbows.

"Oh, I had a terrible night," Nana told me, still rocking. "The candle light vanished. I felt like I was by myself. Why didn't you answer my calls?"

"I couldn't hear you," I responded and looked at Nana's still fearful eyes as tears ran down my cheeks. I cried not only for myself and my family but for all those who loved our country of Bosnia more than their lives, for the millions of my fellow Bosnians who were spending fearful nights hiding in fields, for their burning and destroyed homes, for children who cried in shelters far from their motherland, for orphans without care. I cried for the death of mercy and compassion, consideration and love. In their place ruled hate and cruelty.

Chapter One—Clear Sky

Home ought to be our clearinghouse, the place from which
we go forth lessoned and disciplined, and ready for life.
—Kathleen Norris

My Roots

I see myself as a gigantic fruit tree, with roots connecting the northwestern Bosnia of my father's ancestors with the southeastern Bosnia of my mother's. My mother's village of Zagrade is surrounded by rolling hills that are watered by numerous springs and covered with an abundance of fruit trees. It is a place resembling heaven on earth, a place no one would willingly leave—except out of fear. In pre-World War II Bosnia, many of the villagers spent their entire lives without ever seeing any of the worlds beyond their region. So how did Hatidja Budalica of Zagrade ever meet Mujo Cimirotic of Dubrave? And how did a twenty-one year woman come to marry a widower who was a decade more than twice her age? The Second World War, a war that was especially vicious and cruel in the Balkans, made that meeting and marriage possible.

My mother's village was situated on the border with Serbia. Serbian nationalists formed the Chetnik movement, the Serbian version of the Nazis, intolerant of everyone who was unlike them, especially Muslims. They killed Muslims and plundered and burned their villages. Every night after sunset, all the men and boys from my grandmother's village would run to the woods and stay there until dawn. The girls hid in attics, basements, or barns.

One night, the Chetniks came to my grandmother, whose name was Beida Budalica, and demanded her gold. They beat her. Her daughters, Ema, Alja, Nura, and Hatidja, had to endure hearing their mother's cries as they cowered in fear in the attic. "Darkness crossed over my eyes every time they hit me," my grandma would later say. She gave them all of the jewelry she had - all her rings, necklaces, and bracelets. When they left, Hatidja ran to the home of one of her Serb neighbors and asked them for help. The neighbors slaughtered a sheep and covered my grandma's almost dead body with the animal's warm skin to help heal her wounds.

On a cold winter day a few months later, just as grandma's health was improving, the Chetniks came again. Hatidja, with her mother and siblings—along with most of the villagers—ran the six kilometers to the town of Rudo, arriving in the bitter cold with nothing but the clothes they were wearing.

By the time they arrived, my mother's feet were so cold that she could no longer feel them. The good women of the town dug into the snow, found iced ashes, and put them on my mother's feet. The melting ashes provided warmth, and after several sessions mother began to feel her toes again. Later, whenever my mother would talk about her war memories, deep wrinkles would furrow her forehead and sadness would fill her eyes. "The Chetniks brutally killed everyone who was not able to run. They even killed children," she explained. Her stories were a part of our history lessons. The atrocities were well documented.

The Chetniks and Ustaša, the Croatian fascist movement, were described as demons in our history books. Just across the Sava River had been a concentration camp. On the twenty-fourth of every April our school would organize a field trip to the camp, commemorating that day in 1945 when freedom finally returned to the village. Horrific pictures were on display at the camp, which was designed as a "never again" lesson. After the Second World War, Chetnik and Ustaša leaders were hunted and sentenced for war crimes. When my mother talked about her family's struggles during World War II, I naively thought that such a catastrophe could never happen again. My brain and heart rejected any possibility of war in my dear country of Yugoslavia.

The town of Rudo was so close to Sebia that my grandmother and her family did not feel safe there. With other refugees, they traveled on a freight train for several days from Rudo in Bosnia to Ocucani in Croatia. The refugees ate only a very weak soup made up of warm salt water with a few cornbread scraps in it. Hunger and the bitter cold took many lives. From Ocucani, they walked about twelve kilometers to Dubrave, shivering and cold to the bone the entire way, and there the generous villagers created a camp for them in the village's elementary school.

Mother told the story, "Our life in the school was miserable, but at least we were together—my mother, my two sisters, my brother, and I. Nine families lived in one classroom with only one wood stove. When one family put their bread to bake, another family was already waiting for their turn. We mostly ate half-cooked food. We worked in the homes and fields of the villagers and at the end of each day, the villagers gave us flour, potatoes, or milk in return. Some people mixed water with the milk to make it go further. Late at night, when the other families were sleeping, my sisters and I would heat water in buckets and take it outside to shower so we could rid ourselves of the lice and other insects that made us itch constantly."

During this refugee time, my mother attended one alphabet course in the school where she lived. She learned all her letters and was eventually able to sign her name in cursive. Because her time in class was short, she never really mastered word recognition. But that did not stop her from joking that because they lived in a classroom, she was in school longer than any of us.

Mujo Cimirotic, a Muslim man born in 1892, was a widower with a five-year-old son. He generously opened his home to my grandmother's family. They finally had their own room and even their own stove. Mother, who was born in 1923, was only twenty-one years old when she moved with her family into Mujo's home and immediately caught Mujo's attention with her stunning beauty and strong work ethic. As mother related the story, "He had dreamy, melted-honey eyes and a gentle, ever-present smile. I liked his humor and easy-going personality. He let me take care of his cows and work in his house and fields. I liked his company, and though we did not talk a lot, every time our eyes met my heart skipped a beat, my face turned fiery red, and I hid my gaze. My mother noticed that something was going on between Mujo and me, and she told me to stay away from that old man. But he had a magic power, and I couldn't fight against my feelings. After a few months of this 'courtship,' Mujo asked me to marry him."

Mother chose Mujo to be her husband—and later my father—even though he was my grandmother's age. Grandmother was very angry—the differences in their ages and between their villages were just too much for her. Left without choices, Grandmother later accepted her daughter marriage.

In the spring of 1946, Mujo named his newborn baby

Dervisha, after his first wife. Other people thought that was selfish and offensive to my mother, but Mom liked the name. "'Dervisha' means modest, pious, and someone who opens doors. I wanted my daughter to open the doors of love and peace for everybody," Mother explained. Dervisha filled our father's heart. With her beautiful face, curly brown hair, and big green eyes she was his princess, and he took her everywhere.

Four years later, on May 20, 1950, I was born. My mother named me "Aiša" (pronounced "Aisha"). It means a long, comfortable life, and my mother hoped my name would tell the story of my life. "But I had a hard time delivering you," Mother said. "I was afraid that I was going to die. A wise midwife, Fata Pivach, prayed when you entered this world: 'Dear God, show this girl the straight path, the path of those with whom you are pleased and not the path of those who earn your anger nor of those who walk astray. Merciful God, give her happiness in her life and good people to accompany her wherever she goes.'"

On March 1, 1953, my parents had a son, and Mother named him "Alija," which was her brother's name, but she also liked the name because of its meaning: tall, gentle, and excellent. It was when grandmother heard that she had a grandson that she finally visited her daughter and her family for the first and the last time.

Childhood

The first five years of my life were promising. My father was a beekeeper as well as a farmer. There were not better cookies than the ones my mother made with my father's honey and butter. I always took note when there were a few cookies left after supper, and the next morning, while the house was still quiet, I would follow their smell and they would disappear.

Thursdays had always been special days. Around noon I would wait at the village intersection for my father to return from Bosanska Gradiska. I watched all of the horses and wagons pass by, and when I recognized my father, I ran faster than the wind to meet him. Father would stop his horses and lift me up onto his lap. While he was searching in his pockets for candy, I would snap the horses' reins a little bit and they would start to run. I thought the happiness of my childhood would last forever, but the end was right around the corner.

Several months after my fifth birthday, on January 16, 1956, my life changed drastically. After lunch, while Mother was still feeding my two-year-old brother, my father came into the house and, as he got to the door separating the living room from the kitchen, he suddenly stopped, grabbed the door frame to hold himself up, and called to my mother in a gurgling voice, "Hatidza, Hatidza, I am dying!"

Everyone else ran outside, but I stayed alone in the room with my father. I wanted to go closer to him, but my feet were glued to the floor and I simply couldn't move. Father slid slowly down along the doorframe until he was sitting on the floor. He raised his head, and our eyes met. His lips moved, and he looked as though he wanted to tell me something, but his voice became weak. Suddenly, his head dropped forward, his chin fell on his chest, and he closed his eyes.

A neighbor took me to my uncle's house that night, and the next morning I returned to a house full of people. A white cotton sheet was spread in the corner of the kitchen, and a bowl filled with scrambled cornbread and milk was steaming in its center. Mom was seated close to the sheet with my baby brother in her lap and she motioned me to sit next to her. Her blue eyes were filled with tears and from time to time, as she fed my brother, she breathed a heavy sigh.

"Eat, eat," she said in cracked voice to me, my sister, and my brother. "It is not good that children are hungry when their parent dies." Her words went straight to my heart. My hand became heavy, and I dropped my spoon. *Why is she saying that? Where is my Baba now?* I stood up, walked among the other people in the house, opened the door to the living room, and glanced inside. Someone covered with white sheets was lying on the floor surrounded by serious-faced men sitting in silence. I stood speechless and numb in the doorway. I wanted to walk over to pull back the sheet, but I couldn't force my legs to move.

My cousin took me by the hand and walked with me to another room. After about an hour a large group of people were carrying something green and heavy on their shoulders. They moved slowly. *That must be my Baba. Where are they carrying him?* I looked at them until they disappeared from my view. My feelings of happiness and safety, along with a part of my strength, disappeared with that group of people.

I would never again find candy on my pillow and blanket, never again leave home on Thursdays, and never again find joy in reciting poems and singing songs for our neighbors. At only five years of age I had left the beautiful magical world of childhood for a harsh new world devoid of any luxuries and bent only on survival.

Without father we had no source of income except for a few farming fields, one horse, and two cows. Land was considered wealth at that time, but how would Mother be able to cultivate the fields and care for three small children? She had no farming skills— she couldn't plow or even handle a team of horses. Mother became quiet and frequently dried her tears on the sleeves of her blouse. She would get terrible migraines and vomit every time the postman brought a tax bill levied on the land that father had owned. We had only an old folk-remedy to help her through the pain—potato slices against her forehead and temples, held in place by a tightly wrapped scarf. After Mother recovered from a migraine, she would dictate a letter to Dervisha and then send it to our grandmother in Zagrade. My baby brother and I listened carefully. The letter always started the same way: "Dear Mother and Sister Alja." After several

12

sentences Mother would become quiet and swallow hard. "I don't like to ask them for money, but we cannot pay the taxes. We cannot sell the land. Land is life. It is your future, a present from your father. Selling it would be a selfish thing to do." She was helpless in dealing with these financial crises, and she looked in desperation to us, her children, for the adult advice that we were unable to give.

Those winter nights when our neighbors came to our house holding kerosene lamps were happier. They would take their heavy coats off and sit on our wooden sofa. The women talked with one another while they knitted wool socks and vests and fixed torn pants and shirts. The men would talk about their survival during the difficult times of World War II or their plans for spring. Sometimes they told scary stories about good and bad ghosts that scared us children so much that we couldn't move. Some of them would bring books of folk poems that their sons would read to us.

When we did not have visitors, the three of us gathered around Mother like chickens around a hen. I liked to place my head on mother's chest and listen to her heart beating. A peaceful sound from a burning kerosene lamp and Mother's deep sighs were always a prelude to her stories about her homeland.

"In the place where I was born, mountains touch the sky. The horizon is covered with forests, springs, meadows, and fruit trees. In the early spring, after Djurdjev Day (a Serbian holiday celebrated on May 6), we would pick sweet cherries. As the sun grew hotter during the long summer days, the pears and apples would ripen. During the second half of summer plum season would start. Oh sweet purple delight! We had tons of plums. We made jams and dried them for winter compote. We drank that sweet compote all winter instead of water." My mouth watered as I imagined how good and sweet it must have been, regretting that I wasn't born in that magical place.

"In my homeland," Mother would continue, "water, grass, flowers, air, and animals are different than they are here, and people are different too. They have softer hearts and richer souls."

Winter mornings would start with Mother recalling her dreams from the night before. "Oh, dear God, turn my dream into something that is good for me and my family. I dreamed that I was in my village. My mother and my sisters and I were in the field harvesting the wheat. When we came home, you were all there. My mother was happy that she was able to see you. Oh, dreams."

13

Mother became quiet. "I hope one day my dream will be true, *inshallah*. We need to be patient. God will guide us and fulfill our wishes. God has promised that with difficulty comes ease."

When I was six years old, Mother would wake me before dawn, and I would follow our cows to their pasture, carrying a stick in one hand and fresh baked bread in the other. Our cows bent their necks and grazed on the dewy morning grass. The amazing songs of the chirping birds made me happy. I would sing too, as loudly as I could, believing that my mother was listening and enjoying my singing. On days when large, puffy clouds moved across the blue sky, I watched with fascination their shapes and movements. I would see them form white sheep, beautiful butterflies, happy and sad faces, and flowers.

Almost every night I dreamed my cows were in trouble and I had to protect them. I would often jump from my bed and begin sleepwalking, shouting all the while to my cows, "Sharenka, Rumenka! Stop it! Come back!" Mother would wake me from those dreams. She prayed and asked God to protect me, gently touching my head and shoulders, waiting until I closed my eyes again. I didn't see anybody else who was going to care for our cows, and I was not sure that I would go to school.

School Life

In the middle of May 1957, my mother came to me in the meadow where I was taking care of our cows. Out in the open she helped me change my dress and put on my new tennis shoes, and very gently combed my thick hair.

"You are my big, beautiful girl," she said with a proud smile. "That white building over there is the school," she said, pointing across the meadow to the other side of the road. "You need to go and enroll yourself."

I looked at her, eyes bulging, confused and unsure.

"Do not worry," Mother said confidently. "Your sister Dervisha is in that school. Find her, and she will help you."

"Can you go with me, please?" I asked softly.

"God knows how I wish I could, but who will watch our cows?" Mother paused. "Follow this path, and you cannot miss the school. I know you can do it."

I fell into Mother's arms, and she held me tightly and kissed me. As I walked toward the school, I could hear her prayers fading with the distance, "Dear God, open the good doors for my daughter, and protect her from the wrong doers. You are the great protector."

My mother was right. I found the school and grabbed the knob of the door. I turned it, pushed it, but I couldn't open the door. There was nobody to ask for help, so I began shouting at the top of my lungs, "Dervisha! Dervisha! Dervishaaaa!"

Thankfully, a teacher opened a nearby window. "That door is for the teachers. Do you want to be a teacher even before you become a student?" he asked with a smile. "A teacher will get Dervisha for you."

I was very happy when Dervisha walked me to her classroom. The wooden floor was painted black, and the teacher had a big stick on the desk. *That stick is bigger than the one I use for my cows*, I thought somewhat anxiously. *Is that stick only for bad kids, or do they punish all the students with it?* I didn't like the stick.

"Are you going to be an excellent student like your sister?"

I looked at my sister, squeezed her hand, and nodded.

15

The teacher shifted his eyes to my sister. "Dervisha, are you going to fifth grade?"

"No. My mother cannot afford to pay my bus fare" Dervisha whispered, looking down at the classroom floor. "Mother needs my help in the fields." Tears filled Dervisha's eyes, and I cried too.

The door leading to further education for my sister was closed, and neither our mother nor our half-orphaned selves had the strength to open it. The devastation I felt for dear intelligent Dervisha being forced to bid farewell to an education at such a young age would stay with me throughout my life.

As I stood there with Dervisha, I had no idea that school would become an important part of my life—as a student, teacher, and eventually principal. People opened many doors for me, and when the hinges were rusty and resisted, God sent individuals to oil and loosen them.

Since money was scarce, my sister's old school bag was handed down to me. Mother patched its many large holes, but it was the small ones from which my erasers and pencils spilled out.

Losing my erasers was a disaster for me. I made plenty of mistakes, and trying to rub them off my paper with my index finger only made them look worse. The girl behind me had an eraser that she would lend for a steep price. For the right to borrow it, even if used only for a   single word, I had to give her my lunch bread with its golden-brown crust. Standing in line to get my lunch each day, I gazed out at the trees and houses and swallowed my saliva. Some days, when I was very hungry, I hated this "friend" and her eraser. Still, it was better to deal with hunger than the pain of the teacher's stick.

Losing a pencil was also a serious problem. One day Mom gave me money, and I bought a colorful one. The same day I found that my precious new possession had disappeared! I checked my bag, books, and notebooks, but I couldn't find it anywhere. I took a black crayon and wrote my entire letter "C" worksheet with it. When the teacher saw my messy, smudged work, she asked me to stand up. My throat became tight and tears poured down my face. Luckily the teacher had pity on me and spared the stick.

The end of the school day, I laid my heavy head on my desk and decided to stay in the school I avoid facing mother with the news that I had lost my beautiful new pencil. The teacher heard my sad story and kindly gave me her pencil. My heart filled with warmth, and a gentle smile touched my lips. I thanked her for her enormous help.

When I eventually got home, I told mother the tragic tale of my lost pencil. In response, she bought me a pencil box and a big eraser. The next day my classmate found my new pencil in her book bag. I do not know how the pencil got there, but I was glad when she returned it to me. I placed it in my new pencil box, right next to my big eraser and the pencil the teacher had given me. I was rich. That day at lunch I enjoyed every single bite of my fresh bread.

Math confused me. My brain would absorb information literally. The teacher asked, "If your father gives you two lollipops and your mother gives you two lollipops, what is that equal to?

Sadness touched my heart as she mentioned father and lollipops. I wrote $00 + 00 = 00 + 00$. Everything that was on the left side of the equation equaled everything on the right side. I solved all the problems the same way and turned my paper over, confident that I had done them all correctly. When my teacher handed my paper back, it looked like somebody had killed a chicken on it and nobody saw my grade.

That was not the first time the teacher had left me confused. One day she told us to sharpen our ears. I concentrated very carefully on that task, moved my hair behind my ears, bent my head on my chest, opened my eyes and tightened all my facial muscles. In the middle of this task, as I was pulling hard on my ears to elongate them, she called my name, "Aisa, why are you not listening?"

"I am sharpening my ears," I explained timidly.

"You can relax." The teacher smiled. "Your ears are sharp enough."

One November morning the snow surprised us with a white blanket that stretched to the horizon. I had no boots. To remedy the problem Mom gave me her boots, which she had bought from Maria, the Russian lady who lived in our village. The boots were huge. Their tops reached way above my knees, and my legs looked like black tree trunks. Mom stuffed her wool socks in the toe of each boot and dressed me in her *dimije*. A *dimije* is a traditional Bosnian dress, a cross between a skirt and pants. I could hardly move through the snow as I made my way to school.

In art class that same day we drew a picture of our teacher. I

17

moved closer to the front, so that I could draw her picture better. The *dimije* dragged, the boots clunked, and the teacher remarked, "Next time we will draw Aisa." I was confused. *What would make me so remarkable? Does she like the boots? Leather fur boots were certainly boots only a few could afford.*

During my first summer break from school, while our cows rested in the barn around noon, I went to the mosque four days each week. Without sharpening my ears, I listened to the imam (religious teacher) carefully as he talked about God. Religion became important to me, and I tried to apply that knowledge to my everyday life.

When I completed fourth grade, the village of Dubrave expanded our school up to eighth grade. That summer I noticed changes in Mother's behavior. She was quieter, liked to spend more time alone, and prayed longer. One pleasant evening my brothers and sister were off playing with their friends and I was alone with mother. I could see that she was deep in her own thoughts.

"My dear, it is not easy to be a widow and make decisions alone regarding my daughter's future. These days I've been praying and asking for God's guidance. Every time I ask for His help, the first five verses of the *sura* Clot, which the angel Gabriel recited to the Prophet Muhammad, come to my mind." Mom recited those five verses in Arabic, paused, and translated: "In the name of God, the Beneficent, and the Merciful. Read, in the name of your Lord Who created, created man from a clot. Read, and your Lord is the Most Bounteous. Who teaches by the pen, teaches man that which he knew not?"

"Mother, God wants us to read and write. In school we have to read and write," I said.

"God did not say that only men could read," Mother commented. "Some girls are able to read and write even better than boys. Your old uncle thinks that girls do not need go to school after fourth grade. 'They need only to learn to keep their hands busy with work and keep their mouths closed.'" She paused. "We have two more weeks to make a decision about your education." As she spoke, she gently pulled me closer to her, hugging me with one hand and gently combing my hair with the other. I felt safe and wished I could be in her arms forever.

The last week in August we cleaned the attic, making it ready for the fall harvest. When it was almost clean, Mother said in her soft voice, "Dervisha and I have decided to let you finish all eight grades."

I jumped, ready to fly, and hugged my mother and sister. "Oh thank you, God. Thank you, Mother. Thank you, Dervisha.

"Study for both of us," said Dervisha, with a mixture of happiness and sorrow in her voice. "I want to be proud of you. With God's help it will be possible."

I studied hard after fourth grade and had excellent grades. Eventually math became my favorite subject. My homeroom teacher recommended that I tutor three of my classmates. I gladly obliged. All three of them—Slavica Stanojevic, Branka Lalic, and Zivka Mitrovic—were Serbs, which meant they were Orthodox Christian. But that made no difference to me. We met at my house after school twice a week to study. After an hour or so we would take a short break and have a snack. One day I shared cherries that my mother had bought.

"Cherry trees are abundant in my native village of Turjak on Mount Kozara," mumbled Branka, her mouth full of cherries. "I can pick and eat as many as my heart desires."

"Would you take us there?" Slavica asked.

Branka stopped chewing, and it looked as if fire had touched her face. We stared at her, but she was silent. Slavica repeated her question.

Finally Branka bent her head down and whispered, "You could come, Slavica, and so could Zivka, but not Aisa. You could only come," she raised her head and looked at me, "if you temporarily changed your name."

I was flabbergasted. I couldn't believe my ears and gave Branka a wild-eyed look. This was the first time in my life that anyone had told me I was not welcome because of my name. I looked like any other seventh grade girl in Bosnia, but since Muslims give their children Arabic names, it was obvious that I was Muslim. Slavica meant "glory" in Bosnian, Branka "protection," and Zivka "alive." But the name "Aisa" had no meaning in the Bosnian language.

"I don't want to change my name, and I won't go to your village," was the only reply I was able to compose in my childish mind. "Let's practice math now."

While they worked on our task, I thought, *I am so glad that my parents named me "Aisa." In Arabic my name means "long and comfortable life." A good life is far from hatred, malice, or envy. I am glad to have you four in my home because in Islam helping others and lessening their burdens is appreciated by God more than prayers.*

Branka looked at her lap. The sound of her last sentence still echoed from the room's walls. She picked up her notebook and, as she walked out, left the door slightly open. A brilliant, almost amazing, sunlight entered the room and softened my heavy breathing.

"Come again to our class, Branka," I said, trying to forget her ugly suggestion.

My mother suggested that I go to the vocational high school in Bosanska Gradiska, after graduation from eighth grade of elementary school. She was hoping that I could get practical training in our village grocery store. "You can only wrap yourself with as big a blanket as you have," Mother told me, touching my shoulder with a worn and aging hand that felt like fish skin.

My dear mother surrounded (from left to right) by Alija (my brother), Mujo (my brother Munib's son), and me. This picture was taken 1964.

The Miracles

My dream was to attend a teachers' school, but at that time it seemed impossible.

On May first, Labor Day, just two weeks before my graduation, the sounds of an accordion attracted the villagers to dance, eat, and celebrate the holiday together. The delicate scent of perfume led me to Daya, my aunt's daughter. She was married and had moved from our village to the city of Banja Luka.

"Look at my pretty girl," Daya said as she hugged me. "What is going on with you?"

"I plan to start trade school in Bosanska Gradiska," I shared without any excitement.

"Why wouldn't you study in Banja Luka?" she asked with a smile.

"It's too far away, and we can't afford the room and board," I lowered my voice.

"You can live with my family. As you know, my husband is an army officer, so he doesn't spend much time at home."

"Are you serious?" I looked at her eyes, two glittering stars sent from heaven. "If this could work, I could go to the teachers' school!"

"Go to any school you want. I want to help us have an educated woman in our family."

"Only God knows how much I want to be a teacher," I confided, keeping my eyes focused on hers as I took a few steps backward and began to turn. "Wait, wait! I will be back with my mom in a minute."

With Daya's words ringing in my ears, I ran frantically looking for Mother. It seemed like the door to a magical world had opened, and I was afraid that Daya would disappear and her promise would vanish.

Oh dear God, please help me find Mom! Finally, I spotted her. "Mother, I need you to talk to Daya. Move fast, come on!" I tugged on Mom's hand, talking rapidly. "Daya invited me to live with her in Banja Luka. I could go to the teachers' school. Hurry up! Hurry!" My burning desire to be a teacher must have been from God, and the light of its fire would show me the way.

21

Mom was annoyed but let me pull her in Daya's direction.

Luckily we reached Daya before she left. "Let her go to the teachers' school. I will provide room and food for her," Daya suggested, touching my mom's shoulder.

"I can make butter and cheese—"

"My husband makes good money. I do not need that," Daya interrupted my mom. "I need company. Aisa will be like a sister and friend. That is worth more to me than money."

I was afraid my heart would burst out of my chest from happiness. I was not able to thank God enough for this wonderful news.

Everybody in my village knew that I wanted to go to the teachers' school. In the second half of June, I took the entrance exam. The two-week wait for the results felt like two months.

Fortunately, in the beginning of July I had a good dream. Above the eastern horizon I saw a bright sun. Its rays provided light for me, our home, and our whole village. The sunlight became stronger and stronger until it eventually woke me up.

In the morning I went with the other workers to bundle the wheat on Uncle Nazif's field. As the day progressed, the heat became stronger, and I sweated harder. Suddenly, I heard our neighbor Boro Delic shouting, "Hey, Aisa, you passed the entrance exam. Look at the postcard!"

A chill raced through my body, and I felt as though I had just jumped from the hot wheat field into a pool of refreshingly cool water. But it was not really immersion in water that I felt, but rather the cool satisfaction, pleasure, gratefulness, and delight of realizing an important achievement.

I took the postcard, raised it high, and yelled to my mother, "It's true! It's true! I passed it! Thank God, I passed it!" I ran through the fields like a doe and fell into Mother's arms. Squeezing me, her tears rolled down onto my hair.

"God is so merciful. He answered our prayers," she pronounced with a deep sigh.

"Mom, I want to go and share this wonderful news with our entire neighborhood."

"No, my dear daughter, good news spreads like a good smell. At the end of the day everyone will know about it. Go back to the field and finish your work. Wheat is our food for the whole year."

I was busy again harvesting the golden wheat, and connected the sunlight from my dream with the wonderful news of passing the exam. The happiness that overcame me felt like the light that had covered me, my home, and my entire village in the dream. I thanked God for all of His blessings.

A week before school started, Daya's mother called my mom to her house. When I saw Mother coming back, walking quickly with her head bent down, I ran to our garden to meet her.

"What is wrong? What did Daya say?" I demanded.

"Forget Daya's promises. You cannot go to her home."

I couldn't move. I felt like a bolt of lightning from a clear sky had just struck me.

"How could she betray us?" I could hardly open my mouth to speak. "Is that true?"

"Unfortunately, it is true," Mother sighed. "She can't let you stay because of her husband's job. He has a high rank in the army and can't have anybody in his home except his family. You could overhear and spread army secrets."

"I don't care about army secrets. I only want shelter, so I can go to school!" I cried loudly. Mother cried too, and it looked as though all the vegetables, grass, and birds cried with us.

"What should we do now? School starts next Monday!" I was still sobbing.

"Let me go and talk to your uncle."

"Uncle Nazif can only cry with us," I replied.

A feeling of despair weighed me down as I waited for Mother to return with the awful news that Uncle Nazif could not help us. But much to my surprise, she came back like a fresh spring breeze and interrupted my sorrowful thoughts. Her face was like a full moon, and there was a joyful gleam in her eyes. "We still have hope for your school. I am going to Vrbanja to ask your Aunt Saida to provide a room for you."

I hugged my mother as she prayed, "Oh dear God, have mercy on us. Make a place for my daughter in Saida's heart."

Mother returned from Vrbanja as the sun was setting. "God is great. Your aunt will take you. She said that you are her brother's daughter, and she will provide everything you need just as she is providing for her own children." Mother's words removed the chains from my body, and I was able to move again. A ray of hope warmed my heart.

"We should forgive Daya," Mother decided. "Her role was to open the door of possibilities for you, and that was all."

My dear Aunt Saida would always hold a special place in my heart. She not only treated me as her daughter, but also showed me what true religion is. Four years later, after finishing teachers' school with excellent grades, I told my aunt, "My dear aunt, Almighty God and your family helped me become a teacher. The minute I moved in with you I saw a special light in your eyes, the same light that lit my father's eyes. You have been much more than an aunt to me. If you ever need anything, I'd be glad to do it."

"I'm glad I was able to help you, but you helped me too. You filled the emptiness I have in my soul for my dear, departed brother, your father." My aunt became quiet for a moment and swallowed hard. "I am a widow and have eight children to raise. I will never be able to go to Mecca to perform the Hajj (pilgrimage). If you are ever able to go, please remember me there."

Tears filled my eyes, and I hugged her tightly.

After graduating I was very busy in both my personal and my professional life. I became a full-time teacher in the village of Orahova and married Husein, a young doctor. Our daughter Aida was born in 1974 and our son Samir in 1979. In 1977, I earned a bachelor's degree in psychology and pedagogy, and in that same year I became a high school teacher in Bosanska Gradiska. Until that time I had not felt any ethnic or religious discrimination. I was totally unprepared for the new life that was waiting for me.

Here I am with Husein, Aida, and our friend Persa in Bosnia in 1977

Chapter 2—**Clouds Are Gathering**

Character cannot be developed in ease and quiet. Only through experience of trial and suffering can the soul be strengthened, ambition inspired, and success achieved.

—Helen Keller

Evaluations

In 1980, Tito, the longstanding president of Yugoslavia, died and Serbian nationalism, just like an old vampire, slowly came out of its grave and onto the political scene. The first time I felt its bite was in 1983.

A new law required that all teachers be evaluated by the end of the 1982/83 school year. The principal explained in a teacher's meeting, "We must grade all teachers based on their performance and behavior and place them in one of four categories: Group A, Group B, Group C, and unfortunately, Group F. The last group is reserved for teachers who have failed and will lose their jobs." Some teachers moved their chairs in discomfort, chewing their nails or lighting cigarettes. Clouds of smoke quickly filled the room.

"You do not need to worry," explained the principal, springing up from his chair. "The majority of you will be in Group A."

A few days later I found several teachers in the break room sitting in small groups. They became quiet when they saw me and slowly resumed their conversations in whispered voices. The air, thick with cigarette smoke, was cold, and my greetings, rebounding from averted faces, did not reach their ears. Feeling like I did not belong there, I grabbed my book and headed to the classroom.

One of the young teachers stopped me in the stairway and inquired, "Did you hear what happened?"

My face became still, and my eyes stopped blinking.

"Two of our colleagues were placed in Group F," she whispered in my ear and held her index finger to her mouth for silence.

26

I felt rooted to the step I was standing on, my blouse fluttering to the rhythm of my heart's rapid beats. "Am I one of them?"

"No!" She shook her head and looked up and down the hallway. When she was sure that only the two of us were present, she whispered, "Professor Kozarcanin and Professor Haskovic."

I stood totally confused for a minute. "What did they do wrong?" They were among the last ones I would have placed in Group F.

She shushed me and left for her classroom.

At the end of day, on my way home I joined the same teacher. "Why do the other teachers seem afraid to talk to me?" I asked.

"It's simple," she said just above a whisper. "The two professors in Group F are Muslims, and you are too. Some of them view all Muslims in a negative way, and now that the line has been drawn, they feel justified in ostracizing you."

She blushed, and her voice caught a little bit as she continued. "I heard that both men are cooperating with our enemies. Professor Kozarcanin once belonged to the Organization of Young Muslims. The police even check his home from time to time. Several days ago the police found some pictures there."

"Professor Kozarcanin was imprisoned for it, and that was some forty years ago." I couldn't keep my mouth shut, "Should we punish him twice for the same reason? What has he done wrong in the present, as a teacher? He is only one year from retirement!" I raised my voice.

"I don't know. I am sharing what I heard," she replied, lighting a cigarette and then becoming quiet. It was too late for her to turn back, but she was afraid to go forward. She was a Serb too and uncomfortable criticizing her own.

"What is wrong with Professor Haskovic? Isn't he still in the army?" I sighed. In that time every male was required to serve one year in the Yugoslav army.

"Yes, he is. He even joined the Communist Party while there. People are gossiping that Professor Haskovic has ties to Iran and is supporting its revolution," she reported, exhaling cigarette smoke. "I'm assuming that the principal has some information," she said, surveying the area we were in to make sure no one overheard our conversation.

"How could a young teacher support Iran's revolution at an army base where he has no contact with the civilian world? I'm confused." I shrugged. "As far as I know, Professor Haskovic is Muslim in name only. He never speaks of religion and lives unmarried with his girlfriend." My fingers played restlessly with a corner of my purse. I was frightened, but the thought that God is just and that justice must prevail calmed me.

Walking home from this discussion, I felt cold. Something dark was brewing around me, the same way that clouds gather before a storm, warning us to look for shelter. I ran toward home, seeking the safety and protection of my family.

The next day I met Professor Kozarcanin in the teachers' room where the other teachers pretended to be busy. I went over to the table where he was sitting. "Professor Kozarcanin, I was shocked to hear what happened to you. Is there anything I can do to help?"

"A few days ago the police searched the entirety of my house from the basement to the attic," he shared, shaking his head. "They found one picture of me and my friends taken when I was a young man. That part of my life is now behind me but apparently not to the people who want to do me harm." He was staring straight ahead as he spoke, and only the cigarette smoke of the other teachers reminded us that we were not alone.

Professor Kozarcanin took a pink slip of paper from his pocket and explained, "I have been fired after 29 years of teaching," he paused. "Our principal, Mr. Aliatic told me that my teaching is not based on Marxism. I teach geography. How can geography be based on Marxism? It's ridiculous." He raised his head and looked past me into the distance, as if hoping for justice to come to his rescue. He stood up, looked at his "busy" colleagues, gathered his personal belongings, and walked like a shadow out of the room, closing the door behind him.

A few days later, the principal called a meeting and informed us of the destiny of our "Group F" colleagues. He said the school had no choice but to dismiss them. "The police had Professor Kozarcanin's 'records,' and the Communist Party had classified information about Professor Haskovic."

The meeting brought many surprises. Professor Smolic raised his hand and then shared, "We work with these people, but we really do not know who they are, what organizations they belong to, and what harm they might cause to our students or to us. We should always be on guard against them, so that they cannot spread their ideas, like a many-armed octopus. Our enemies might lead our students in the wrong direction."

"They should be ashamed," another voice shouted. "They do not appreciate all that their country has done for them. Shame on them! This school has no place for them."

Other people commented loudly, condemning these two men who, until a few days ago, had been their friends and colleagues.

Our office clerk, Milja Hrabric, raised her hand and said softly, "We have to be careful here. I have known Professor Kozarcanin for years as a very good and polite instructor. He wants to work only one more year, until his retirement. I heard that the police found one very old picture. Is that the reason for his dismissal? We could be making a mistake here."

I admired her for her honest warning, but her words tapped a hornets' nest, and angry hornets from all around the room stung her. But her words had come from her heart, and she did not flinch.

I am a coward, more concerned about keeping my job than seeing that justice is done. My sense of guilt guided me to think about the Aesop fable, "Three Bulls and a Wolf." In the story there were three bulls on a meadow that were continually menaced by a hungry wolf. But the bulls, rather than joining together to defend themselves against the wolf, scattered, each looking after his own safety. The first time the wolf came, it killed one of the bulls while the remaining two were happy to be alive, rejoicing that now each had half of the meadow to itself rather than a third. When the second bull was killed, the remaining bull rejoiced, but then the wolf came after him. Together they could have defended themselves, but separately they were easy targets.

A few months of nervous uncertainty followed. Professor Kozarcanin had lost his lawsuit. I was frightened. *How are innocent people able to protect themselves?* I thought. *How could a judge decide the case without demanding facts? When would the police come to my home to search for "evidence" of my activities?*

Professor Haskovic eventually came back from the army and reported straight to school for work. When I asked him about his place in Group F, he replied, "I can't believe this happened to me when I was serving our country. All their information is gossip and lies." I could hear the anger in his voice and see it in his eyes.

"Who started the gossip?" I asked.

"One of our colleagues surprised me with a visit. She was interested in me romantically. I introduced her to the officers as my girlfriend so I could get the day off." In the army, a private would get 24 hours off duty if a significant other or close family member visited. He continued, "At the end of her visit I thanked her and mentioned that I had a stable relationship with my girlfriend. She became upset, fabricated a story, and reported me to the Committee of the Communist Party. They checked my army activities and my student life, and I have proof," he said stabbing the desk with his pencil, "proof that I am innocent!"

He stood up and paced in the room. "I will protect my rights. I cannot be a bone for those hungry dogs to play with. The school representatives will pay for all their mistakes. Muslims must have the same rights as everyone else in this country." He paused. "I've never encountered more hatred towards Muslims than here. Some of our colleagues are absolutely blind with hate. They are waiting like hungry wolves to kill unprotected sheep. I hope I am wrong, but I fear that you will also feel it soon."

Professor Haskovic filed a lawsuit and I was glad for his victory.

All the unpleasantness of that school year and all the negative energy it generated wore me down. Over summer break I spent time with my family and worked in my gardens and orchards. These activities restored my spirits and my energy.

In mid-July, one day when I was downtown, I meet Sherifa, a fellow teacher. Her smile disappeared as she asked me, "Did you hear about our evaluations?"

I shook my head. "No. Where are you and I ranked?"

"We are in Group C, the lowest group we can be in and still keep our jobs, just above Professors Haskovic and Kozarcanin. All those drunks are in groups A and B. Even the professor who has been accused of a sexual relationship with a student has been rated above us." She spoke faster and louder.

"Why didn't the principal inform me? Where is the list?" I could feel my skin burning like hives breaking out.

"It's somewhere in the school," she shared, pausing for a

moment. "Go there and check."

I was dumbstruck, unaware of the July heat that was beating down on us. I headed straight to the school and went to the principal's office. Our principal was the only other Muslim besides the four lowest rated teachers.

"I heard that the evaluation list is finished," I said with an edge of anger in my voice. "I want to see where I rank."

"I don't know where the list is," he responded, glancing up from his desk. "A teacher's place on the list will not have any effect on salary." He looked down at the papers on his desk.

"My place is important to me." My emotions were rising and began to fuel my anger. "I heard that I am in Group C, just above professors Haskovic and Kozarcanin. What is it about my teaching that caused you to rank me so low?" I stood straight like a soldier.

An ocean of rage was coming from his eyes. "You have no appreciation for the fact that you have a job!" he screamed. "We couldn't put all the teachers in Group A. We are all capable of improving our performances. What difference does it make if you are evaluated on par with Professors Haskovic and Kozarcanin?" The sweat was running down his forehead, and there was spittle at the corners of his mouth.

"I don't support my country's enemies," I voiced, defending myself.

He opened his eyes wide, came around the desk to me, and said almost in a whisper, "Remember, those two professors did not support any enemies either. Our enemies are in this town and in this school. Go home and be thankful that you even have a job."

He returned to his desk, sat down again, and went back to shuffling his paperwork, dismissing me without the courtesy of a single word.

I was shocked. My principal, a man I had worked with and respected, had disappeared. In his place was a diminished man I didn't recognize. The chair, it occurred to me, was fitted with wheels that the wind could blow in any direction. Just now the wind was blowing him in the direction of self-preservation.

For the first time in my fourteen years of teaching, I did not want to go back to work at the end of the summer. I wanted to be home and remain there with my family, my gardens, my orchards, and my fields. The only bright spot was my students—young people

31

I respected and trusted. With them I had built a special bond.

Some teachers noticed the injustice and tried to correct it nominating me for a principal's position.

Ups and Downs

Five years later, in 1988, we needed to elect a new principal. I did not have any ambition to be a school leader. Surprisingly Mila, the language teacher, emphasized my honesty, hard work, fairness, patience, and consideration as reasons for my nomination. In an atmosphere saturated with dense Serb nationalistic smog, I wondered why she had nominated me. I accepted.

Since my success was the result of my reliance on God and my selfless work, I was able to perform well in my new role. During the three years that I served as principal, three of our students won first place in the Yugoslavia physics competition and then won third place in the European competition in Stockholm. Our small school in Bosanska Gradiska was third in all of Europe! I was proud of our students and the majority of our teachers. More than ninety percent of our students were passing. Our school won first place in the entire region in the number of students enrolled in different sports, music, art, and many other extracurricular activities. Many of our graduates had continued their education in different colleges, not only in Bosnia, but also in Serbia, Croatia, Austria, Germany, and the United States.

In the spring of 1991, our school applied for the title of *gymnasia.* A gymnasia is a step up from a regular high school with a rigorous curriculum offering students the strongest possible foundation for college. The entire community wanted to have gymnasia in our town. As the school principal, I was busy making sure our equipment met the gymnasia requirements. Additionally, my son Samir was finishing sixth grade, and I hoped a gymnasia education would be available to him after he graduated from elementary school.

On Friday, May 17, at the end of my workday I heard footsteps running down the hall and a quick knock on my office door. Persa, a Serb colleague, slipped into the office and quickly closed the door behind her. She looked disturbed, even fearful, as she leaned close to me and whispered, "I couldn't sleep at all last night. I don't know how to share this information." She took a seat, pushed her hair off her forehead, and said softly, "A group of our faculty members came to my home last evening reeking of beer. They talked about you." She was picking up a piece of paper from my desk to hide her gaze. "It is really ridiculous, but a Muslim cannot be a school principal anymore. 'This is Serb territory,' they said, 'and Serbs must have all the leading positions.' They don't trust you anymore." She raised her head and lowered her voice, "They want everyone at the school to forget that you are a friend. Last night I defended you, so now they hate me too. One of them was ready to attack me physically."

I looked at Persa's panicky eyes and felt fire burning my cheeks. *And getting rid of me as principal is not the only thing they might do to me. Are Chetniks appearing again?* I was quiet, feeling like I was in a flood with the murky, swift water carrying me and everything I knew downstream. I questioned my belief that people couldn't develop hatred without a reason. "We've worked together for fifteen years. They elected me as their principal three years ago. What did I do wrong? I was Muslim all along."

"I tried to reason with them last night, reminding them how well our students have done under your leadership and how our salary has never been higher, but some of those drunk teachers did not let me talk. They were rude, shushing me and cutting me off in the middle of sentences." Her face blushed, and she stood up. "They have already decided to place, as a transitional principal for the summer, Professor Lazarevic."

"I'm sorry that politics has entered the school," I remarked, sighing. "I am thankful for the good that has taken place in my three years as principal. All the inspection reports were very good." I shifted my gaze to the papers on my desk. "But, if Serb nationalism grows, they will remove me from the school completely."

Deep in Persa's eyes I could read fear as she waved her finger quickly back and forth. "It cannot happen here. You have us, your friends. Don't worry." She left the office.

The chemistry teacher, who was the staff meeting leader, opened our teacher conference. Mila raised her hand, cleared her throat, and announced, "We are going to create a very important school for us and future generations. It is an enormous step for our small community, bigger than we could imagine." She paused and looked at all of us. "We need to nominate an experienced teacher who has the reputation, knowledge, and ability to lead us toward prosperity and progress. I am sure that I share your opinion that the best candidate for the position of interim principal is Professor Lazarevic."

Silence filled the room. Professor Lazarevic, with a gentle smile on his lips, didn't look surprised. He moved his hands in front of his face and said, "Wait, wait, our colleague Aisa is our current principal. That means we have two nominees. We should vote."

Sanja, a young biology teacher, whispered, "Why do we need to choose the principal for the transition period? I am confused."

"It is okay. I'll talk to you later," I whispered and raised my hand. "I want to ease our work and keep our unity. We only have one candidate for the interim principal position. I am voting for Professor Lazarevic."

Sanja touched my elbow. "Why are you doing this? I'll give you my vote. I hope many teachers will do the same."

I placed my finger to my lips and said, "All of this was planned weeks ago. This meeting is just for show and to make the changes official and legal."

The next morning the superintendent of our area's high schools, Ostoja Gvozderac, a very good leader, called me to his office. "I heard what happened at the meeting at your school last night." He was in a rage. "We have some crazy people here. You successfully led this school for three years, and they want another principal for the summer? I cannot understand it."

"This is the perfect time for me to return to teaching. I could enjoy my summer break and start the new school year in the classroom. I really like students." Persa's words were echoing in my ears as I continued, "Everything in our life is temporary, changeable. We want something, but it may not be good for us, or we may not want something, but it is good for us."

Mr. Gvozderac shook his head. "You can see it as you want, but for me it is disrespectful and ridiculous. Some of them are—I do not have words to describe their behavior." He stood up and paced the room." The state inspector, Damir Beatovich, is coming tomorrow, and I need your help to establish the new school."

"I'll be glad to help."

I had hidden my hurt. Being a principal was stressful, and I would be glad to get back in the classroom, but being pushed out was painful.

Inspection

Mr. Beatovic, arrived at our school around 10 am. When he finished his work, he looked through his papers and disclosed, "We checked all of your equipment. Our board will make the final decision about your gymnasia soon."

The superintendent looked at Mr. Beatovic and said with a soft smile, "Our entire community and all of our employees really want the new school. Our current high school is very well recognized for its astute students. We have knowledgeable and hardworking teachers who are enthusiastic and determined to motivate our students to study as much as possible." He paused, lowered his voice, and asked, "If we need your help in getting the new school, perhaps a phone call, we can get in touch with you?"

The inspector said in strong voice that he would be more than happy to help us establish the new school.

The next morning I rode my bicycle to work while analyzing the events of the previous day. The spring flowers along the route were fragrant, and I was at peace. The quiet of the school was welcoming. I had no meetings scheduled, so I worked on assigning judges for the entrance exams.

The school secretary called me, in an almost demanding tone, to come to the meeting room. A strange group of people startled me as I entered the room. Blagoja Secerovic, the mayor's secretary, was biting his lower lip and pacing in the room. He supported his chin with his right hand and clenched his left fist. He constantly wrinkled his forehead and looked out the window. Mrs. Prashnjevic, the local school inspector, massaged her scalp above her ears and sighed from time to time. Her hair stood up wildly, giving her the look of someone who had ridden a motorcycle backwards or had tossed and turned sleeplessly throughout the entire night. Mr. Radulovic, the half-drunk principal of the vocational school, was talking to himself and moving his fingers.

They didn't pay attention to me at all. I stood next to the door. *What is going on here? Where is the superintendent? Is he alive? How many people died?*

Suddenly Mr. Secerovic turned toward me and shouted from

the top of his lungs, "Mrs. Softic, how was your meeting with the state inspector yesterday?" He looked like a coiled snake ready to apply its poison.

I instinctively stepped back and said, "The meeting? The meeting was fine. The inspector said ..."

The secretary stepped forward and, waving his finger in my face, threatened, almost in my ear, "Listen to me. If Gradishka does not get its gymnasia, you cannot live in this town! Do you hear me? You cannot live here!" He was red in the face, and the blood vessels were bulging on his neck. I moved myself a few steps back to keep him at a more comfortable distance.

Mr. Radulovic stood up and sandwiched himself between us, facing the secretary. "Mr. Secerovic, don't worry. Please don't worry. Let me solve the problem. Let me handle it, please, please." He stood like a shield in front of me, and I felt a little safer behind his back. "Inspector Beatovic and I are close friends. We are like this." He crossed the index and middle fingers of his right hand and raised them. He spoke with a drunken slur.

I noticed Mr. Secerovic fold his hands as if he were praying. "Oh, brother Radulovic, can you help? Save our lives? Look what Mrs. Softic did to us. Look at this disaster!"

The school secretary jumped in front of Mr. Secerovic and patted his shoulder. "Mr. Secerovic, Mr. Secerovic, I have good news for you. Mrs. Softic is our principal for only a few more weeks. We named Mr. Lazerevic as our interim principal, but we must take care of the legal formalities in order to make his appointment official." He cleared his throat and continued, "I must admit Mrs. Softic was a terrible principal. Can you imagine, Mr. Secerovic, she was reading a newspaper while I was presenting the laws and regulations for the new school? It is evident that she doesn't care for the new school at all."

Mr. Secerovic turned and ran toward Mrs. Prashnjevic. "Why did you keep Mrs. Softic in the principal's position for three years? Three long years. Why? It is your responsibility. You are the school inspector. Yes, it is your mistake," he shouted. "Everything is your fault!"

"I am sorry," the inspector almost cried, "I felt sorry for Mrs. Softic, I pitied her."

A chilly silence filled the room. I leaned against the wall for a moment to collect my strength. *Oh my dear God, please protect me from these lies. You are the best protector. How can they do this in front of me?* I rubbed my eyes. *Can I trust my eyes and my ears today? How could Mr. Secerovic be so cruel asking Mrs. Prashnjevic why she didn't remove me from my position? Am I a chess piece that they can move around where and when they want?* I narrowed my eyes and saw Mrs. Prashnjevic as a string puppet in a children's show. *Are you sorry for me or for yourself? You had the nerve, in front of the half-drunk principal you have always complained about, to say you were sorry for me! How many times did you come to me to vent when you couldn't even find him? Did Mr. Secerovic really say that I cannot live in this town? Is he going to throw me out of my home? Doesn't he understand that the bricks in our home came from the clay of my ancestors' land? We built our home with our own hands. Doesn't he understand that a part of my soul is in my house? Does he want me to be a refugee as my mother was almost fifty years ago? Oh, no, no...*

The school bell announced the beginning of a class I was required to teach to meet my principal's teaching requirement. Walking toward the room was like walking through thick, heavy mud. I loved teaching, and my daughter was in this class, but the day's events were just too heavy on my soul. Slowly the students' bright eyes helped me feel better. My daughter waited until all the other students had left and then asked me softly, "Mother, what happened? I couldn't concentrate at all. Your eyes told me that something terrible must have happened."

My heart ached again, and the tears came. "You are right. Some people hurt my feelings, but I am fine now. I'll talk to you at home," I shared, quickly wiping away my tears.

After that terrible meeting I needed fresh air like a dry garden in August needs rain. I left the school and turned right onto the Unity and Brotherhood Bridge. My eyes took in the slow-moving muddy Sava River, a dirty reflective surface, separating Bosnia and Croatia. *All of our lives are moving like water in this river,* I thought. The river was flowing slowly, glittering from time to time, carrying gray cedar logs and white birches, and eventually curving and disappearing in the distance. It was a warm spring afternoon, and the coffee shops lining both banks were crowded with the young people who would, for better or worse, inherit what our generation left for them.

I leaned on the bridge rail, still warm, and felt the sun's rays touching my face. My heart seemed to skip a few beats when I saw the second floor terrace of the Kozara Hotel. The joyful memories of that building were real and present once again, and for a few moments I recalled New Year's Eve celebrations and youthful parties. A gentle wind whispered in my ears as I recalled the fast, rhythmic music of those bygone days. Once again, I saw those young dancers and their feet hardly seeming to touch the ground as they moved to the music.

Sava River is flowing slowly, glittering from time to time and disappearing in the distance.
I liked to observe the river and its surroundings.

Even my feet had moved as I thought of the past. But the echo of the secretary's words, "You cannot live in this town," brought me back to the present and made me stiff. I hugged my legs and placed my head, suddenly heavy, on my knees. As I slowly became calm again, my heart began to beat in rhythm to the sound of the river's lapping waves. My ears caught the sounds of the animals and insects in the large park behind the hotel, and I melted into nature for a moment and became a part of it.

My skin chilled when the chords of church bells and voices from minarets beautified the ambience, each calling its faithful members to the worship of the one God, greater in mercy, knowledge, wisdom, compassion, love, and justice than all of His creation. I stood out of respect for God's greatness.

How could the strange company from this morning choose to be a slave to other humans and allow their happiness to depend on the whims of their bosses who controlled them through fear and injustice? This very morning I had witnessed what the human marionettes were willing to do to please their masters. If they would only surrender themselves to the one God, they would be able to shield themselves from fears and insecurity, and they would be able to use the gifts and guidance that God offers them to spread mercy, justice, love, and truth in order to make a life of peace.

The sun in all its glory was sinking in the west, and I left the bridge and walked toward the main street. The street was filled with slow moving elderly people. I smiled, remembering that my teenage daughter and her friends called the street "Elephants' Trail." They avoided that street because their behaviors were scrupulously examined by elderly walkers and compared with youth behavior of a half-century earlier.

I met several citizens who were discussing serious topics with worried looks. Everyone talked about war, but my heart and my mind couldn't accept the imminent catastrophe in my dear Bosnia. A wind played gently with my scarf, wafting it out like a flag. *A war is impossible in my Bosnia unless another country attacks us,* I thought. The three main nationalities—the Orthodox Christian Serbs, the Roman Catholic Croats, and the Muslim Bosnians—all lived together peacefully and respectfully.

The Dream Country

Throughout the entire following summer I prepared Aida to be an exchange student in the United States. My husband, Husein, was scared to send our seventeen-year-old daughter to an unknown world by herself. "How can we help her if she has problems over there?" he worried.

"Life is unpredictable," I replied. "We can only ask God to protect and guide her." The Naser family of Carlisle, Ohio—Kathy Naser, a teacher, her husband Naggy Naser, a technician, and their two daughters, Leila, Aida's age, and younger Nadia—had written Aida a welcoming letter. On our way to Belgrade's airport, Aida, Husein, Dervisha, and I listened to on car radio a free concert for peace from Sarajevo. That city had always been a hub for musicians and artists. The songs of those beautiful young voices singing in unison were hopeful and inspiring. Calmness came over me as I thought about the possibility that politicians could find peaceful solutions to their problems and that our country might not be facing war. When it was time for Aida to board the airplane, Husein's chin trembled, and tears filled his ocean blue eyes. My sister dried her cheeks. I hugged Aida calmly, asking God to protect her.

My sister looked at me astonished. "Do you have a heart or a stone in your chest? Your husband is crying, but I can't see tears in your eyes. Are you the mother of that child?"

"I am going to miss her, but I am at peace about this trip," I explained.

Watching Aida's light brown hair swaying gently on her shoulders as she walked away to board the plane, I said softly, "I believe God sends his angels to protect those on their journey to find knowledge, and He is opening the door of blessings for my daughter and for our entire family. I am confident in His protection and in His mercy, so I do not have to cry."

Dervisha looked at me. "I admire the strength of your faith. It is blessing to reach that level."

That night, the unnerving sound of the slow-moving tanks, like the tolling of a church bell, filled the streets of our town. A chill ran through my body as I thought about Ernest Hemingway's *For*

Whom the Bell Tolls. I asked myself, *Is the bell tolling for my town's residents, for our freedom? Are those soldiers and their weapons making us safe?*

After only a few hours of sleeping, the gentle lights of dawn appeared. That morning many children gathered around the tanks and talked to the soldiers. My neighbors were hoping the soldiers would protect us. I went downtown, but the empty streets surprised me. Suddenly a parent of one of my students called me, "Mrs. Softic, it is dangerous to be here now. Go home as soon as possible. Airplanes are going to drop bombs on the bridge soon. Go, go!"

I rode my bike back home as fast as possible; and as soon as I entered my house, the loud sound of an airplane scared me. We locked the house and shut the blinds. The telephone rang. Hesitant, I finally picked up the receiver. "Mom, I arrived in the United States. America is beautiful. I'm doing fine. Don't worry about me at all. I like my new family. I will write a letter to you soon." Aida's joyful voice lowered my fear of the airplanes, bombs, and earsplitting noises. "Thank God you arrived safely. I am so glad you made it."

Her letters, which began arriving shortly, were full of exciting and good news about her new life. Reading them to myself several times and to everyone who asked about Aida, I almost heard her voice, saw her smiles, and felt her excitement. I was glad that she was so far from our war-prelude troubles.

Kathy, Aida's host mother, Aida, me, and Husein in the Indian Museum in Dayton Ohio 1991.

The Attack

You never know where danger is lurking. In the beginning of 1991/92 school year, for safety reasons our students were relocated to the village schools. On November 28, 1991, on my way home from a relocated school in Nova Topola, I decided to stop in my dear village of Dubrave and pay a short visit to my sister's and brother's families. As I got off the bus and the sound of the engine faded, I entered into a frighteningly deep silence. The cold wind brought drops of rain and the sound of rifles. I covered my head with my scarf, secured my purse, and put my hands in my coat pockets. The village where I had been born, had grown up, and now visited weekly, had become a strange place. The villagers, the majority of them Muslims, peaceful and hardworking people, had always kept their doors open to all guests and visitors and shared their food. Now they were locked in their homes. Even the houses, with their blinds pulled down like cataracts over a person's eyes, looked fearful. The evening sky was a dark gray with not a gleam of moonlight.

"It makes my flesh crawl thinking about how you are going to your home," my brother said. "At twilight we lock our doors and become prisoners in our own houses."

"This village is the most beautiful place on earth to me. If I were in need, all the villagers would come to my aid," I responded smiling.

As I returned to the bus station, Serb army trucks moved on the road pulling strange machines behind them. Several soldiers, carrying weapons on their shoulders, walked on the other side of the road. Their strange, shadowy faces filled my heart with fear.

The wind played with my wet scarf and brought with it the frightening chatter of rifle shots in the distance, so I did not hear the soldier's steps until he was just three meters from me. The air around him reeked of alcohol. I stepped down from the sidewalk and looked at the brown grass trampled by human feet in front of me, hoping that he would pass. He stopped just in front of me and asked in a heavy Serbian accent, "Do you know where the community office is?"

I glanced at that tall, dark stranger with his broad, willow-colored face and groggy eyes. His brown hair stuck out from beneath his uniform hat and spilled down his forehead. I was confused. *He must know that all government offices are open from 7 a.m. until 3 p.m. Does he want to know if I am from this Muslim village? What should I say?* I took two steps away from him. *If I answer him, perhaps he will leave me alone.* My eyes were glued to the rifle on his shoulder when I replied, "The community office is in the old school building. Turn left, and in a few hundred meters you will see it on your right.

I was silent, waiting for him to follow my directions, but he did not move. His unwelcoming presence created a whirl of emotions inside me, and my heart beat faster. An approaching car shed light on him, and I noticed that his face was creased but not wrinkled. He could have been a few years older than my daughter. He frightened me with his bulging eyes and strange face. I tied my scarf thinking, *Why did you come here from Serbia? Go home and live a peaceful life.* Suddenly, he grabbed my jacket and pulled me close to him. I froze, unable to move for a moment. He bent his head and rumbled in my ear, "Are you Muslim?" A terrible fear, as if straight from a nightmare mixed with the bitter cold paralyzed me. After a few seconds my eyes darted frantically, looking for anybody who could help me, but the street was empty. I moved his octopus hands off me.

"Listen to me. Go there." He commanded, stretching his index finger toward a bench, and huskily murmured, "Don't be stupid. Do what I tell you to do."

I opened my eyes wide, pushed him with my elbows, and took a few steps back. Car lights were approaching, and I frantically waved both hands signaling for the driver to stop. The car slowed down but passed. "Oh, no, do not go! Take me!" I panicked as I desperately searched for another way to get away from the beast. He grabbed me again. His strong hands were like an iron grip on my shoulders. The cold rifle touched my face. "Are you crazy? If you don't go there immediately, I'll kill you! Do you hear me? I'll kill you!" He looked like a monster. The alcohol in his body made him unstable, and I seized an opportunity, pushed him hard, and ran faster than I even knew was possible. *You can kill me, but you cannot make me feel awkward or embarrassed. I will not let you make my soul or my body dirty. I did not come to your country. You came to my village to wreak havoc.* Every muscle in my body stiffened, expecting a bullet from his machine gun, but I ran. My whole body was numb. I still ran. I could feel him aiming at me, but I could not bring myself to look back.

I searched for any protection, any word or act, to survive. By God's grace, at that moment I saw high-beamed headlights and a taxi sign on the top of a car. I ran into the middle of the street, waving both hands in the air. *Dear God, please stop this car before a bullet comes, please, please! Protect my body from those hands!* The tires squealed, the taxi stopped, and the driver opened the door.

"Take me! Take me, please!" I pleaded, jumping into the car. I closed the door, and the car moved. "Go! Go! Hurry up! He is going to kill me!" I covered my ears with my hands, lowered my head below the window, feeling more like a culprit than a potential victim.

The driver, glancing back at me, asked, "What happened? Who wants to kill you?"

"The soldier, the soldier that was there," I hesitated looking at my still-trembling hands. "I was ready to be hit by your taxi rather than fall into his hands again." Even after a short break I found it hard to explain what had happened. My lips were glued to my teeth, and my tongue barely moved. A cold sweat covered my shivering body. I felt a terrible headache coming on.

The driver looked at me and said something very strange, the last thing I would have expected him to say. "When that soldier's mother from Serbia sent him to war in Bosnia, she never thought that he would attack a civilian woman coming home from work." The driver shook his head. "If he had killed you today—you are a woman like his own mother—how could he have lived with your blood on his hands?"

His words calmed me, and I thanked him. When we reached my home, the driver walked me to the front door and spoke to Husein. Husein frowned, and I felt his trembling hand on my shoulder. I noticed Samir's watery green eyes, and tears slid down my face. I hugged my son tightly, and my sobbing penetrated the quiet air of our neighborhood.

My stomach ached, and a sharp pain hammered my head. Samir, only twelve years old, sat next to me. He put his head on his knees and hugged his legs. While touching my fingers, his twinkling green eyes came nearer, and he asked, "Mommy, why did the soldier want to kill you?"

"He was drunk. He did not know what he was doing," I replied softly, thinking what a tender heart my son had. "I am constantly asking God to protect us. The soldier couldn't use his rifle at that moment because God protected me."

I couldn't sleep that night, and when the house was quiet while my family slept, I sat on a chair and lifted one of the blinds on the window. As the moonlight illuminated the diplomas and the jewelry on my dresser, I thought how, in the blink of an eye, all of that could lose its value. A hush filled my soul as I thought of the village cemetery across from the mosque. Tonight, without God's protection and the courage of that taxi driver, my soul and body could have been in a totally different place. I prayed that our troubles would be over, but the political situation in Bosnia was deteriorating on a daily basis.

Chapter 3—**The War**

A great war leaves the country with three armies—an army of cripples, an army of mourners, and an army of thieves.
                                    –German Proverb

The Bloody Spring and Summer

In the death of Yugoslavia, Bosnia paid the biggest price. In 1991 after only three weeks of war Slovenia became an independent country. In Croatia the war lasted longer. Serbia and Croatia wanted to divide Bosnia. In the beginning of 1992, the Bosnian government let its citizens decide their future and conducted a referendum. The referendum asked: "Are you for a sovereign and independent Bosnia and Herzegovina, with equal rights for all citizens—Muslims, Serbs, Croats, and all other nationalities that live there?" More than 90 percent voted for independence. On March 1, 1992, Bosnia became an independent country, just like Slovenia and Croatia, the other republics of the former Yugoslavia.

Serbs abstained from voting, arming themselves instead. We watched the news at seven-thirty every night, changing channels nervously and listening to different broadcasters, latching onto any glimmer of hope that sanity would prevail. In the beginning of April, Yugoslavian journalist Goran Milic said on television: "I wouldn't have much faith in people who promise you that instead of a single shared house, you will each live in your own. I don't believe them because first you'd have to build two new houses while the people who are making these promises are destroying the only ones we have. And when all of us are left without a roof over our heads, forming long hopeless convoys of refugees, when our children are begging European observers for powdered milk and chewing gum and our daughters and sisters are making love with soldiers from exotic countries for two or three dollars, don't say: 'We did not know,—how could we have known!' We must all find the strength to inform our leaders of the things we don't agree with."[2]

---

[2] Senad Hadzifejzovic, *War: Live on Air* (Sarajevo: Senad Hadzifejzovic, 2002), 32.

The first victim of war is the truth. Serb radio presented the situation to its people as if they were the victims, oppressed and marginalized, fighting for their survival—the complete opposite of the truth. Fear is the most potent tool, our primal instinct, pulling one group together into survival mode.

Radovan Karadzic, President of the Serbian Democratic Party, said, "There's no such thing as a united Bosnia and Herzegovina." I didn't believe him. *Bosnia will survive as well as the Bosnian people,* I thought. I couldn't sleep nights. Bosnia was part of me, my homeland. How could these people be dividing our land? I thought of all the bloody images I'd seen on the news, and my heart ached as I thought about all the families that were displaced and all of the people who had died already. I asked myself, *Why are the extremist wing of the Serbian Democratic Party and the Serbian Radical Party destroying Bosnia, their own homeland, and killing everyone who loves her?*

The Serbian army mobilized every man living in Bosnia between eighteen and sixty years of age. A man who refused to be a member of the Serbian army would lose his job. How could Muslims join the Serbian army? It was very sad to see those men go to work only to be turned away in front of the factories and other work places, forbidden to provide for their families. They looked like the Jewish people did during the Second World War. The only thing missing was the yellow Star of David armband.

When it was obvious that Bosnia was sinking into war, Husein called Aida. "You cannot come home. Fighting has already started in Sarajevo and in several towns in the east. We will send you many articles from the newspapers stating that it's too dangerous for people here. Do not worry about us. We love you."

After a few weeks, the Serbian army decided to use those unemployed men as their slaves. They were forced to report every day to an army headquarters where they would be given work detail assignments. Some of them cleaned the town streets while others cut down trees, cleared wood, dug trenches, or worked in the fields of Serbs.

Late one afternoon the phone rang, and I recognized the voice of our friend Hamida. "We need Husein's help. I'll be glad to see you too."

Husein picked up his doctor's bag, and we walked quickly to Hamida's home.

"My son Enes is waiting for you." She wiped her tears and placed several pillows under Enes' head, helping him into a semi-sitting position.

I hardly recognized Enes. His face was swollen and bruised, and his right eye was completely closed. His hands were bruised too.

"One of my former classmates beat me up today," Enes whispered, gasping as he spoke. He looked at his mother to help him tell his story.

"He was working the fields close to the Sava River with the other Muslims who refused to be mobilized for war," explained Hamida, wiping her son's face. "His former classmate, a Serb in uniform with a rifle, was their boss. By the end of the day he recognized my son and asked him about his life. Enes told him that he had earned a bachelor's degree in biochemistry from Zagreb University and that he was married and had two sons..." Hamida's tears prevented her from further explanation.

Enes gathered his strength and continued softly, "He then asked me why I had not joined the Serbs' army. I said that we both had our jobs to do. Suddenly, the soldier's face became as red as a stop traffic light, and he said that he'd show me what his job was and that I couldn't be anything other than a *balija* (a derogatory term for a Muslim)! He shouted and beat me harder and harder. I tried to protect my head and face with my hands. I fell to the ground and was unable to get up. My co-workers carried me home." He put a wet towel on his forehead.

Hamida and I left the room while Husein examined Enes. "We have to leave our home as soon as possible," uttered Hamida in a shaking voice. "How can Enes go back to work? That soldier could kill him. I can't stand it." Her tears prevented further conversation. I looked through the window and even the gray sky shared our heartbreak. Hamida raised her head and looked at her grandsons' pictures on the desk and whispered, "It is good that his wife went with their children to visit her mother in Croatia. At least they are safe there."

"It looks like your bones are fine," we heard Husein's voice. "You can take some medicine to relieve the pain and help you relax for tonight. Tomorrow you need to see the doctor to excuse you from work. I don't think you should go back. Your classmate is crazy."

"He is not alone," whispered Enes. "It looks like their soldiers are competing to see who is best at mistreating us. A few days ago one of us had a chicken drumstick for lunch. A soldier ran over and kicked his lunch several meters away from him. He said that meat was not for *balijas*."

"I wouldn't be able to control my anger," Husein protested.

"If you don't, they would kill you and then say it was self-defense," Hamida responded.

We left Hamida's house when the sun was disappearing and the dark had started to cover our surroundings. After a few days Enes collected all the required documents and left his home.

Almost all of the grocery stores in our community had shortages of cooking oil, detergent, coffee, and cigarettes. I waited in line for hours just to buy a liter of oil, and sometimes, just before I got to the front of the line, the last liter would be sold to the person ahead of me. The Serb soldiers occupied our unfinished weekend house in Orahova's hills.

Spring was bringing the brown grass back to life, and warmer air helped the tulips and cowslips open their flowers and share their pleasant smells, but the war-related destruction brought fear and worry to my heart. Even the songs of the birds sounded cheerless. I worked hard in our fields and planted seeds in every foot of our land. That work gave me hope for a better autumn, and helped me sleep through the nights.

My 53 years-old brother, Munib, became sick that spring. Becoming weaker every day, he stayed in bed most of the time. I prayed that he would recover, but on April 23, 1992, his heart stopped completely.

I spent that night with his family, sitting in a corner next to his wife, Fata, mourning his life cut so short. Memories from my childhood flooded my mind.

For Munib and Fata's wedding Mom had bought me new shoes: brown, shiny, and my size. How exciting! I kept them under my pillow, taking them out only occasionally for a few minutes enjoying my imaginary world. The day before the wedding, I couldn't wait any longer and wore my new shoes to school, my eyes glittering with happiness. This was the first time I had a pair of hard shoes of my own, shoes that actually fit, and I was proud to show them off. When I came home, I washed the clay from them and set them in the center of the oven, just like bread, to let them dry.

After a few minutes the kitchen was full of smoke. When I opened the oven door, there were my beautiful shoes looking like hungry baby alligators with their mouths wide open. I screamed, "My shoes. Help. Help! Is anybody here who can help me? Anybody?"

On the wedding day, nails from the burnt shoes pricked my feet and made walking extremely painful. I gritted my teeth and climbed into the carriage. Once I sat down I felt much better and covered my shoes with hay. When we arrived at Fata's house, everyone else left the carriage to eat, dance, and sing. When I tried to move my feet, the pain from the nails was too sharp, so I stayed in the carriage. A woman came three times to invite me in, tempting me with candy and good food, but I lied, saying I was not hungry. When she walked away, I pulled more hay around me to stop shivering in the afternoon cold.

On the way to our home we passed the cemetery where my father was buried, and my eyes filled with tears. *Dear Baba, it's been four years since you left us. I am tall now, so it would be hard for you to lift me. I am an excellent student in the third grade. I will go to school for only one more year, the same as Dervisha. Munib promised to support me in my schooling, but I am not sure that it will be possible. I am sorry that you are not with us today to celebrate Munib's wedding. The bride is pretty.* I paused and wiped my tears. *I miss you!* I lifted my cold hands, recited the first chapter from the Qur'an, and asked God to give my father a good place in heaven.

When we arrived home, I didn't waste any time putting the baby alligator shoes in the garbage and putting on my old rubber boots. Then I joined my family and enjoyed the festivities in comfort.

I remembered when my brother, Munib, asked me to read Cinderella, my favorite story. All our family was happy.

"I will support you to finish all the schools in the world," Munib had proclaimed in a voice full of admiration.

I was perplexed. *Will I still be a student, even when I am old and gray? For how many years will I study? How many schools, and where would these schools be?*

I also remembered the letters that I wrote to my brother while he was in the army. I regretted that recently I had not spent enough time with him and his family, but I hadn't expected him to die so soon. I was confident that he knew he was my dear brother and that I loved him. I lifted my hands, recited the opening chapter from the Qur'an, and asked God to give my father, my mother, and now my brother a good place and that we would meet again in paradise.

A few days after the funeral I packed some food, took my bicycle, and headed to our field in the village of Dubrave. I hoped that we would have enough wheat and potatoes, so we would not be hungry. On my way I thought how my home village had become farther away because I couldn't drive our car anymore. Gasoline was too expensive and difficult to buy.

It was a cold, cloudy day that reminded me more of late fall than spring. The wind played with smoke from Dervisha's chimney, pushing it down and lifting it high. It was a sign that she was cooking lunch for me. I worked enthusiastically until a thunder-like sound disturbed the field's peacefulness. I raised my head and saw Dervisha coming from a distance.

"It took me a long time to finish cooking lunch, so I couldn't come earlier to help you," she explained as she put the fresh food and her hoe down. "It looks like I came a little too late. Did you hear that strange sound?"

I nodded eating her delicious food. "I'm not sure where it's coming from. Are those bombs, or is it distant thunder?" I said, keeping the plate of food on my lap. As the sound became stronger, we looked at each other with growing fear. Rain started to drizzle down.

"Let's go home," Dervisha announced and walked toward the road. "It looks like there is going to be a downpour." She turned her head toward me. "Give me your hoe and go straight home. You must be more careful. Don't think about the fields these days. Take care of yourself and your family." Her words mixed with the music of rain as I pedaled hard for home.

When I got home, the electricity went out, and I lit a candle. The siren of a missile attack sounded just as we finished our meal, so we moved to the basement. Suddenly, a strong explosion left us deaf for a moment, and our entire house shook and rattled. I took Samir's hand, came closer to Husein, and covered us with a blanket. I raised my head and checked on Nana, my husband's mother, who'd been a part of our household for the past twenty years. She was sitting on her sofa and whispering prayers.

"It looks like a missile passed over our house and exploded in our garden," reported Husein. "Give me a candle, and I will go to check."

"Wait a little bit. Another missile could come," I asserted and listened to his steps going upstairs, passing the balcony doors, and then coming back in the cold darkness.

"It looks like it just missed us. I can't see any damage to the house."

"Thank God we survived," I remarked, feeling my very rapid heartbeats.

The telephone interrupted our silence. I hardly recognized Mina's shaking voice whispering, "Did you hear what happened?" Before I answered, Mina said, "Elvis died. The missile exploded in Djevad and Ilinka's front yard and killed their son, Elvis."

I froze, unable to move or talk. I pictured Elvis, a cheerful, handsome teenager with beautiful blue eyes and a pleasant smile, playing with my children and helping me out in my garden. And now, in an instant, a missile had passed over our home and killed him.

"Aisa, are you still there? Did we lose connection?" Mina asked.

"I am here, but I cannot believe what you just told me. My mind cannot accept it," I uttered with a broken heart.

"Unfortunately, it is true," Mina cried. "Djevad's family went to their basement when they heard the siren. Elvis went to get some candles. He was on the steps when a part of the missile hit his head. His family rushed him to the hospital, but he passed away."

"How can we help?" I asked.

"They are still at the hospital," explained Mina.

My legs became heavy, and I walked slowly toward Samir's room and sat next to him on his bed. I looked at his innocent face, and tears poured down my face. The tragedy that happened only a hundred yards from our house could have occurred in any of our homes. *I don't know how Ilinka is going to be able to deal with her loss*, I thought. *When it comes to the safety of our children, a mother's heart is like a fine crystal glass, easily shattered and impossible to mend.*

All sounds ceased. Standing close to the window, I looked at the neighbors' house. Memories of their dead son flooded my mind. My heart was full of sorrow for Elvis, his parents, his siblings, and all of us who knew and loved him. I shivered. The sky was bursting with bright stars. I collected my strength and prayed, *Dear God, please help Elvis's parents. I am asking You from the bottom of my heart to protect all children. Open the door of your mercy and stop wars and killings.*

The next day many people came to the funeral to pay their respects to Elvis. He would be forever missed.

Through the summer of 1992, sadness and worry became my constant companions. The Serb military besieged Sarajevo. The people who were trapped in the city were starving. All those people—my dear Aunt Nura, her family, my Aunt Ema's two sons with their families, my cousins, other relatives, and good friends— were trapped inside, all innocent civilians. They were hunted like wild animals by snipers wherever they moved. A sniper killed my cousin Mehmed Mashanovic. He left behind his wife and three children. I cried for days over that tragedy.

Muslims from the nearby town of Prijedor, from its suburbs, and from the village Kozarac, were taken to the Omarska concentration camp, and only a few survived.

The special Serb units called Scorpions were a source of fear in Muslim and Catholic villages and in our neighborhoods. They would come to Muslim and Croat's homes under the pretense of needing to search for weapons. Some Serbs took the opportunity to profit and offered guns for sale. Considering the circumstances, some Muslims bought them. Serbs would report those that purchased guns, so Scorpions would visit their homes.

Many Muslims in our town and other Muslim villages were killed in their homes, in their yards, on town streets, and in market places. The Scorpions took Hashim Hatic from the village of Dubrave, and he never returned. Many young men such as Elvir and Mirsad Fajkovic, Enes Zahirovic, Emir Dervisic, Ismet and Bajazit Mulalic, and Jasmin Lovic were killed, but nobody found their dead bodies.

One hot day Dervisha called me and through her tears told

me that Scorpions had taken our brother, Alija, to the police station as part of a weapons investigation. I grabbed my purse, took my bike, and went to the station as fast as possible, picturing my brother with bruises and covered in blood.

I questioned myself as I approached the police station. *How could I, a powerless Muslim woman, help my brother? How could I protect him? What could I do?* All of a sudden I remembered my mother's advice: "Always seek God's help. God says, 'I am as my servant expects Me to be, and I am with him when he remembers Me. If he thinks of Me, I think of him. If my servant comes to Me walking, I go to him running.'" *Dear God, protect my brother; give him the tranquility and the strength to explain his innocence.*

I walked swiftly through the hallways of the police station. All the faces looked stern. Finally, I recognized one policeman as a former student, and I came fearfully to him whispering, "Can you please check on my brother? He is here somewhere." I looked around and lowered my voice. "A policeman took him from his house and accused him of possessing weapons. I am a witness that he does not own any weapons."

My former student nodded, and after a few minutes he came back and disclosed, "Your brother is being released. He'll be with you soon."

"Are you sure that you found my brother? His last name is Cimirotic, not Softic," I whispered nervously with tears in my eyes. My heart was beating hard, and my palms sweated.

"Your brother is okay. The policeman only talked to him."

Every minute lasted an hour. Finally, I heard steps and met my brother's fearful eyes.

"How did you know that I was here?" Alija inquired with surprise.

"Dervisha told me. I was scared they would beat you or take you to jail," I said, searching for bruises on his body.

"Somebody told them that I was planning on making weapons, so they brought me in for questioning."

"Who would spread such a lie?" I asked, astonished.

"A few days ago, I was joking around with some guys from our neighborhood. I was saying that in this economy the only profitable thing would be to make weapons. I can't believe that one of them took me seriously and reported me to the police. You never know who your enemy is."

"The police pay people to give them tips on potential traitors," I warned. "You must be very careful about what you say and where you say it. Remember that a war is going on. It's no time for jokes."

I invited Alija to come to our home to relax, but he wanted to go home to his family.

Fear was everywhere. On Saturday morning, August 8, as Husein left for work, I heard gunshots. At first I thought it was the Serbs just firing in the air, which is what they did most of the time. But when the shooting continued, lasting for hours, I became worried. Suddenly, Mina, my next-door neighbor, came to our house shaking. "Some young men from Dubrave and Orahova are fighting the Scorpions on Poloy."

"Have they come there?" I looked at her in surprise.

"They swam across the Sava River to Croatia and returned back with weapons. There are casualties on both sides. This is not good for us. Serbs will take revenge. They will come and kill many Muslims." Her voice was about to crack. "Lock your door, and don't go outside. Keep Samir in your house."

I locked the front door, still thinking about the new information when the clucking of my chickens reminded me that I hadn't fed them yet. As I took some of their food and stepped outside, I heard a car stop suddenly in front of our house. My blood froze, and I hardly breathed when I saw five soldiers come around the corner of the house and approach me.

"What are you doing?" The soldier's voice sounded as loud as a lion's roar.

"I am feeding the chickens." I looked at the chickens' empty feeding dish.

"Why is your garage door open? Who is there?" another soldier asked, and a huge cloud of fear beamed from his eyes.

"The garage is empty. I just opened the door to take out the food for our chickens." I walked toward the garage. "I am going to lock it right now." I walked toward the garage.

"Go inside your house!" They headed back to their car and left.

I ran into the house and pulled down the curtains. As I washed my hands, the telephone rang, and I recognized friend of

58

mine, Goranka's whispering voice. "There are soldiers in our town everywhere. It is not good for Muslims to be on the street. Don't leave the house. I'll bring you bread and milk if you need it. If you have any problems, give me a call."

I only needed food for the chickens, but I did not mention it. I was confused. Many questions crossed my mind, *What is going on? Why did the soldiers stop in front of my house? How long will we be locked up in our home?*

My stomach protested as I took a bucket, went out through the basement, and slowly walked into the garden. I carefully listened and glanced everywhere. The sound of weapons and human steps made me shiver, and I tried to hide myself among the tall corn.

I recognized my neighbor, Ilinka. "Did you hear the terrible news?" she whispered. "The Scorpions did not know that the young Muslims had weapons. They came too close to them, and 18 Scorpions died. My sister-in-law said that tomorrow night, after the Scorpions hold their funerals, they are going to kill all the Muslims." Ilinka barely spoke above a whisper, so I couldn't hear her well. "What are you going to do? Where are you going to hide?" She was coming closer to me.

I shrugged.

"I hope my sister-in-law is going to help us," Ilinka said. "Her husband is Serb. For me it is a little easier. I am not Muslim, but I am worried for my husband' cousins, you, and all of our neighbors."

"Husein is working today and tonight," I responded, pulling weeds around a corn stalk.

She moved closer to me. "Can you ask some of your Serb friends to protect your family in their home tomorrow night?"

The idea was totally strange to me. "No, I will not. I will be in my house with my family. Why do they need to come to kill me? What did I do wrong?"

"I only want to help," she expressed apologetically. I gave her several peppers, and she left.

When I came back, Nana noticed my concerned look and told me, "Don't worry. It is better to put our trust in Allah and ask Him for help. If the whole world were to come together in order to help you, they would only be able to do so if God wanted it that way."

The reassuring energy came back as Nana's soft voice

59

penetrated the silence. *It is so good to have Nana with us*, I thought. *She asks for God's blessings for all of us. Dear God, hear our Nana, and fulfill her wishes.*

As the sun settled in the yellow-red western sky, the weapons became silent. The light disappeared from the horizon and a deep darkness covered the entire community. The air, saturated with fear and moisture, was hard to breathe. It looked as if hell had opened its door, ready to grab and swallow our entire town. My ears, like antennas, detected the sounds of several cars in the street, and a strange thought came to my mind: *I am not sure if we will survive this war in this place. My mother was a refugee. It looks like our destiny.*

The roosters, announcing dawn, interrupted my thoughts. I walked to my balcony and sat among my big plants, thinking about what the gentle dawn light could reveal in pushing the night darkness away.

The Risky Outing

I noticed Husein walking home slowly with his head bent. He entered the living room and confided softly, "The last twenty-four hours were the busiest in my life. I was helping a nineteen-year-old soldier whose kidneys were injured. I am not sure that he is going to make it. The whole night he called out to his mother, asking her to help him." Husein became quiet for a while. "If I had any power, I would stop all the wars in the world. It is heart-breaking to see the young die. Their lives have just begun."

As Husein went to sleep, I shook the empty bags of chicken feed and ended up giving them all of the bread in the kitchen. I walked aimlessly through the house, afraid to ride my bicycle the six kilometers to get the chicken feed, but also scared to watch them go hungry. Finally Samir and I decided to ride our bicycles to get some ground corn.

An eerie silence surrounded us as we entered the empty village of Dubrave. My mouth and throat were dry, and I could hardly push the pedals.

My sister was wide-eyed when she saw us. "You rode your bicycles this far? We are too scared to go to our barns to take care of the animals. The special police have been patrolling the streets all day yesterday and today." She served us lunch and brought out a bag of cheese, a bucket of milk, and two big bags of ground corn. We placed all these on our bikes along with two bottles of fresh, cold water. It was difficult to pedal the heavily loaded bicycles in the scorching summer heat.

As we got about halfway home, I noticed three black spots moving in the distance. I wiped the sweat from my forehead and looked again. The bike stopped, and my feet touched the road. I clearly recognized three soldiers approaching us.

They could take away my son. Oh no, I cannot think about that. What should we do? We could leave the bikes and run into the cornfield. But then the soldiers would take our bikes and search for us in the field. Could we push our loaded bikes into the cornfield with us? We wouldn't be able to move quickly enough through the field. The soldiers would notice and kill us. Should we go back to

61

Dubrave and stop in front of one of the houses? If the villagers saw soldiers behind us, they wouldn't open their doors. Dear God, I ask You by Your mercy, by Your knowledge, by Your wisdom, by Your power, and by Your other great attributes to protect my son and me from those soldiers! You are the best of protectors. I couldn't move.

Samir stopped and, turning his head, inquired, "Mother, what is wrong? Is your tire flat?"

"No, come back and I'll tell you," I whispered. "Look, three soldiers are approaching. What should we do?" My hands became cold.

"Mother, we should continue to ride our bikes. We will be fine. Even if they recognize us, we didn't do anything wrong. We have food for ourselves and our chickens. They can check our bags," maintained Samir confidently.

Meanwhile the soldiers were about twenty-five meters from us, and we could hear their conversation. It looked as if they were sharing jokes and laughing loudly. I told Samir to go first, and I followed him. I grabbed the bike tightly and prayed, *In the name of God the Merciful, Benevolent. Dear God, pour Your mercy on my son and me and protect us from any troubles. Make our legs strong, and make this journey easy for us.* I repeated the prayer until my mouth and my chin became numb. When the soldiers came closer, my hands and legs turned to stone.

I decided to greet them. I moved my lips and fearfully glanced at them. They looked at each other and continued to talk among themselves as if they did not see us at all. When I could no longer hear their boots, the burden on my chest disappeared, and my legs and hands came alive again. I thanked God for all His blessings. It looked like the soldiers didn't notice us.

Samir declared, "I told you. We will fine."

I pushed the pedals with all my strength, and in about twenty minutes we arrived home. Our entire flock of chickens had gathered next to the fence. After eating their food, chickens moved their wings and made happy sounds.

The Fearful Night

After supper I went to the garden behind our house, looking for a place to hide. The hot dry air promised a warm night. The sky was cloudless and blue. Nothing looked promising, but the orchard looked like a safer place than our house.

When I returned to the house, I waited until Husein looked up from his book, and I communicated, "It looks like we are going to have a terrible night. Serb soldiers are going to kill many Muslims in revenge for their dead friends. We could spend the night in the orchard."

"What are you talking about?" My words had surprised Husein. "I worked all of last night, and I'm not going anywhere."

The sunlight disappeared from the horizon. The night brought fear along with its darkness. I walked through the house unable to find a safe place. Nana, moving her prayer beads, was asking God to keep us safe.

"Nana, how did you survive the last war?" I asked, sitting close to her.

"During the Second World War we left our home twice." Nana began. "The first time we stayed at a refugee camp in Croatia for a week. We didn't have enough food, and my shoes broke. I returned home barefoot, and I was happy to have my own place again." Nana paused. "The second time we were refugees for several months in the village close to Dubica. We brought flour and corn from home, and cooked and ate with the other refugees. My rubber shoes were fine during this second time as a refugee. When we went back home, we found an empty, partially destroyed house. Thieves stole everything, even the wooden floor boards. It took several months for us to repair it."

Suddenly, the sharp sound of an explosion shook our house, and Nana became quiet. We looked at each other silently. Explosions came again, again, and again, louder and louder. My heartbeat pulsated in my ears. The sound of nearby machine guns made us deaf for a moment. Looking fearfully at Husein, I asked, "What do we need to do?"

He peeked through the blinds looking out at the street. I joined him. It looked like a stormy night without a break between the lightning and thunder. Fire from burning houses reached the sky.

"The sounds of catastrophe are coming from downtown. We should go to the room facing the garden," I asserted, moving blankets and pillows. "Samir, bring our shoes to the room, please.

Nana's shoes are under her bed. If we must run out, our shoes will be ready."

Husein called Nana to come with us, "It is safer for us to be in the other room. All of us will be together. A bullet can come through the window into your room."

"Thank you my son, but I am fine here, with God's help," responded Nana, remaining seated, moving the prayer beads. We were able to see her face dimly lit by the candlelight.

As the three of us moved to the room, we heard a shotgun blast from the closest street. Samir's face became pale. Glancing fearfully at both of us, he exhorted, "Let's go to the basement, outside, or hide somewhere. Are they going to kill us tonight?"

Husein put his hand around Samir's shoulder. "We cannot do much. We don't know where a grenade might explode, but I am sure that nobody will throw one at us." Husein paused. "They have weapons, and they are showing their power."

I left the room to call Nana gently again, "Nana, please come to the room with us. We are frightened for ourselves and especially for you all alone in your room. Your shoes are with us."

She clenched her prayer beads in her fist and replied softly, "Don't worry about me. I prayed to God and asked Him to bestow His protection upon us. People threw the Prophet Abraham in the fire. God made the fire pleasant for him." I stood, astonished by Nana's words.

After midnight the gunshot fire slowed and the night became quieter. Nana rested in her bed peacefully. Samir slept. I sat next to him and gently touched his curly hair.

Husein put out a candle. "It seems that we are sinking deeper and deeper into this horrible war," Husein sighed. "I cannot see an end in sight. I'm frightened at the thought that we might become another Palestine."

"I can't believe that war could happen again. It looks like a continuation of World War Two," I mumbled.

"I found in Dedier's memoir that Muslims were the second highest group of people killed in that war, just after Jews. Nobody talks about that." Husein shared with worried eyes.

"I will pray and ask God to finish this war as soon as possible."

I placed a light blanket on Samir's back and legs, and went to bed but couldn't fall asleep.   Mother's stories from the last war flooded my mind until dawn.

Soldiers Blocked the Entrance

A dull sound woke me up at seven the next morning. I lay for a moment trying to figure out the origin of the sound. As the knocking continued, I put on my robe and made my way to open the door. To my shock, there stood Zehra, Husein's cousin's wife. Her red eyes and a swollen face communicated her feelings before she said a word.

"My husband, Ramiz," she expressed in a rush. "The military police took him to jail yesterday. I didn't sleep all night. His mother would die if she found out."

"Come in. Come in," I urged, ushering her inside and following her into the living room.
"Why did they take him?"

She sat down, dried her face, and raised her sad eyes. "A Serb soldier, someone we had befriended and thought we could trust, came to our house yesterday with three soldiers. He asked for the weapons. Ramiz gave him the four rifles we had bought from him. The four of them knocked Ramiz down and began kicking him and demanding more weapons." She dried her face. "How could he give them something he didn't have? I cried and asked them to leave my husband, but they dragged him to their car and drove him to jail in Banja Luka for questioning." Zehra couldn't talk. "Can you go with me to find an attorney?"

I hugged her. "Of course I'll go. Let me make coffee for Nana, and I'll be ready soon." I went to the kitchen, prepared the coffee, and hurried to my bedroom to get dressed.

As I laid out my clothes, I heard the front door hinge squeak. *Who is coming in? I locked the door.* I grabbed a nightgown and ran down to the living room. To my surprise my husband was standing just inside the door.

"Husein, what happened?" I walked quietly toward him. "Are you sick?" I looked at his pale face.

He sat on the chair supporting his head with his hands and explained, "Some soldiers blocked the hospital entrance. They checked our ID cards and stopped all Muslim and Croat employees from going in." He paused, and our eyes met. I read confusion, fear, and hopelessness in his gaze. "Some Muslim doctors, realizing what was going on, left immediately to avoid the humiliation. It was awful." Husein was breathing heavily and repeatedly slapped his right thigh with his useless ID card.

"Why? You worked for twenty-four hours on Saturday." I was shocked.

He shrugged. "I need to see my patients, but I fear that Saturday, August 8, 1992 was my last work day as a physician."

Soldiers blocked the hospital entrance. They checked the employees' ID cards and stopped all Muslims and Croats from entering the facility.

I sat next to him, both of us distressed. "It must be temporary," I said. "The director will call you back shortly. Who will administer the dialysis?" I stood up and massaged his shoulders. "And we have another problem," I continued. "Zehra is here. Ramiz is in jail in Banja Luka."

"Oh, what a distressful day! Why is my cousin in jail?" Husein rose from the chair to walk to see Zehra.

After explaining where her husband was and why, Zehra dried her face and continued, "The Serb army ordered the men of Orahova to clear the fields and treated them worse than wild animals. They beat them and forced them to drink urine. We hardly recognized them when they came back from work. They beat our cousin, Osman Softic, until he fainted." She looked at both of us and lowered her voice, "My husband invited the officer in charge of the work detail to our home for a drink and supper. He asked him what we should do to survive this war. 'Disappear,' the officer responded.

'There is no way that you Muslims are going to please the Serb establishment. Our territory must be cleaned of you!' He said that while sitting at our table and eating the food I had prepared for him!"

While Zehra spoke, I recalled the Serb officer Baracia, whom I had met at one of the congressional meetings I attended when I was a Social Democratic Party representative. He wore a uniform, but his partially buttoned shirt revealed scars on his lower neck. It looked as if somebody had tried to kill him. "My army went quietly to the village of Orahova," he had said. "But the village is full of Muslims, people I personally hate. Our soldiers are doing a good job there." *And there we were: Cousin Osman and other men had been beaten, Zehra's husband had been hauled off to jail, and my husband and other Muslim and Croats medical workers had been denied entrance to the hospital where they worked. Was this the "good job" that Baracia was bragging about?*

Husein frowned and stared, remarking, "Are we going to make it? God only knows how many people were killed last night. The town looked devastated this morning."

"We must leave this country. It is the only way to survive!" Zehra's voice rose. "My sister-in-law, Sadika, and her family are refugees in Austria. They live in peace. She found a job in a hospital. Her husband has the medical help he needs for his kidneys. Their children go to school. Look at us! I am trying to find a way to get my husband out of jail before they kill him." She stood up and walked toward the door.

The summer heat pressed down on Zehra and me as we left the house. The air was still. The grass and flowers were wilting from the heat and lack of rain, just as the Bosnian people languished from discrimination and the brutalities of war. The town's empty streets were hardly recognizable. What had been a thriving business section was now rubble. Broken bricks and smashed glass littered the streets. The word *Kristallnacht* came to my mind.

My eyes and Zehra's met in disbelief. Sweat glued my blouse to my body. We walked forward, avoiding bricks and rubble.

A Serb woman, also a resident of Bosanska Gradiska, came toward us. She whispered, "Look, our soldiers destroyed their own town. It is a shame on all of us." She surprised me. "It was a terrible night. I heard my neighbors, recognized their voices, but couldn't help, couldn't open my door, couldn't move. If the soldiers knew that I was trying to protect Muslims, they would kill me." She became quiet for a moment and then added, "I am afraid that God will punish my people."

Zehra left her and walked toward the office of Mr. Stanic, the attorney. I thanked the woman and then joined Zehra.

When Mr. Stanic heard Zehra's problems, he replied, "It is not easy to aid your husband now." He paused before continuing, "But Dr. Softic helped my mother while she was ill, and I feel an obligation to help his family. I'll go to Banja Luka and see what I can do. It will be very difficult, and I can't make any promises."

I thanked Mr. Stanic, and then left him and Zehra to work out the details.

Once I emerged from the office, I leaned against the building, wanting to go home, but curiosity led me to see if soldiers controlled the school entrance. I walked a few yards in the school's direction with my heart beating harder with each step. *Oh no, I have to go home and help Husein with his heavy load. The hospital was closed for him. Is this the end of his career? Is this the death of his doctor's work, his knowledge, and his experience? No, that's impossible. Do they know how hard Husein worked to become a doctor?*

I turned around and went home with warm tears rolling down my face. Husein and Samir were asleep in their rooms. I sat carefully on the edge of our bed and felt my eyes drawn to the face of the man I had known and loved for more than two decades. *Will the local military headquarters assign him to dig trenches for the Serbs, to clean the streets, work in a field?* My hands trembled. *Dear God, please help us. I am not sure that we can pass this test. This load is too heavy for our weak shoulders. Please have mercy on us.*

Between Fires

What would we do if I were turned away from my school the same way that Husein was turned away from his hospital? We would both be unemployed and unable to find work because of our Muslim faith. How would we survive without an income?

I grabbed my bicycle and headed to school. When I arrived at the building, I stepped down from the bike and searched carefully all around the yard. I kept my ID card in my sweaty hand. The school door was slightly opened, and I checked carefully both left and right, but nobody was there. I sharpened my ears for heavy steps following me. I glanced behind me and noticed a tall soldier with a rifle on his shoulder. My hands shook, ice touched my heart as I looked at his weighty boots.

Opening the office door, he called my name, "Aisa, did you sleep well last night?"

I raised my head, and a cynical smile covered the face of the teacher from the vocational school, my colleague Nickolas. I looked at his boots again.

"Did you see how we fought our enemies? They haven't received all of what they deserve yet. Last night was only the beginning. We have to show them our teeth—ha, ha, ha!" His belly shook as he laughed.

I looked for the secretary to defend me, but in her chair sat Freda, one of our young teachers. Freda stood up, placed her right hand on her hip, and walked toward me. She raised her eyebrows, almost touching each other. "Yes, colleague Nickolas, we did not know what our enemies were able to do. We worked with them and trusted them. They killed our children. We should not show any sympathy towards them! Shame on them!" Her words sounded louder than the school's bell. I opened my eyes wider to be sure that the same people I used to know were really in front of me.

She came closer to me and lowered her voice a little bit, "We cannot live together any more. We don't trust you. We are now in different worlds."

"Don't worry, colleague Freda," Nicolas smiled. "I guarantee you that they'll receive what they deserve."

I was caught between two fires. I couldn't open my mouth. I wasn't about to argue with them, especially with Nickolas standing there with his rifle. *Where am I? Did I come to the same school where I have worked for fifteen years? Are these my colleagues? Why is Freda so angry? Wasn't she my friend?*

The entire office became tight for me. I dried my sweaty forehead and only sighed deeply. We all became quiet, and I was afraid that they would start launching verbal insults at me again. I asked about the schedule for the first workday. Freda gave me the paper without looking at my face. I left the office.

The school building was spinning around me, so I sat outside on the steps. The hot summer sun warmed my body, but my heart was cold as ice. I lowered my heavy head to my knees. The Brotherhood and Unity Bridge caught my eyes. My tears blurred the letters. I stood up, took my bike, and slowly walked home with Freda and Nickolas's words still echoing in my ears. Knowing that patience is the companion of wisdom, I told myself that I must stop and think before reacting.

As I walked past the bus station, I noticed Zehra waiting there, red-faced and looking at the bus schedule. "Are you satisfied with the lawyer's help?" I whispered to her, not wanting any other ears to hear my words.

She raised her head, shrugged, and replied softly, "I don't know. I need to talk to my husband. If the lawyer helps release him, I am ready to give him all of our money." She cleared her throat. "Pray for our entire family." She paused. "I am planning to go to the jail in Banja Luka every day. I am afraid for my husband's life."

When the bus came, Zehra got on it and departed. As I rode home, I remembered my grandmother's long walks to Banja Luka during World War Two. She made the journey each day to visit my Aunt Alja. An airplane had dropped a bomb in Mujo's farmyard and had torn a huge wound in Alja's left leg. People quickly gathered, covered the wound as best they could, and took Alja six kilometers away to Gradiska's hospital where a doctor looked at the leg and sent Alja immediately to the hospital in Banja Luka. The doctors recommended amputation, but at this point grandmother's courage took over. She refused. It was war, and she could not stay in the hospital with her daughter. So each day Grandmother walked forty-two kilometers one way from Dubrave to Banja Luka to, in her words, "Keep Alja's leg alive."

Every morning after early prayer, Grandmother placed a

bottle of water and a piece of bread in her scarf and walked to Banja Luka arriving around noon. She stayed with her daughter for about two hours, washed her face, prayed, asked with her tears for Allah's help, and looked at Alja's leg. She came back to the village around sunset reciting all along the way all the *surahs* (verses) from the Qur'an that she knew. She begged Allah to heal her daughter's leg. *Alhamdulillah* (thanks be to God), He saved Alja's leg—a true miracle.

I hoped the miracle would happen again, and Zehra's husband would come back home safely.

Cyrillic Permanent Alphabet

After a few days the school year started with many changes. On the first day I recognized my Cousin Nafa's blue Mercedes parked in the school's lot. *Why did she come to the school?* I thought. *All her children have graduated. Is she waiting for me?* After I parked my bicycle, I saw my colleague Borislav Smolic get out of the car. He was wearing a military uniform. I quickly bent over, pretending to be fixing my sandals, and ignored him, hoping that he would not notice me. *He went to jail last fall for sexually assaulting a student and was supposed to be serving a three-year sentence. His teaching license was revoked indefinitely. How can he be free and at school?*

I went into the teachers' room as quietly as I could. My colleagues were busy hugging and kissing Mr. Smolic. He laughed as he described the fighting around Sarajevo. "They don't have any chance of surviving. All of Sarajevo will soon be ours," he shared with a beaming smile on his face.

"What about Ilidza? How long before we get that part?" a new teacher asked.

"Don't worry about Ilidza," Smolic entreated proudly. "It belongs to us now. Soon all of Bosnia will be ours, and we will unite it with Serbia. All of the Serbs will live in one state, one big Serbia," explained Smolic arrogantly. The teachers, applauding, looked at him admiringly.

"Did you hear what President Karadzic said?" Smolic asked. "Every soldier will have ten hectares of land and a few hectares of woods. And our President always fulfills his promises."

The principal opened the door. "I am pleased to greet you and wish all of you a happy and successful new school year. I am glad to share the amazing news. You can see our colleague, Mr. Smolic, is with us. I personally welcome him. Mr. Smolic will be our employee, but as you all know, he teaches self-defense, so he will be more with the young soldiers than with our students. Welcome back, colleague Smolic!" The principal delivered the last sentence loudly and clapped his hands. Mr. Smolic stood up, and the entire room echoed with applause.

"Thank you, my dear friends, thank you, thank you," he said, bowing his head and looking around the room like an Olympic athlete with a gold medal around his neck.

I became sick and looked through the window. I didn't belong there, and Mr. Smolic was not my hero. I still remembered the first time our student Nada and her mother had come to meet me. I was still the principal. Nada had stuttered, "Pro—Pro—Profff … Smo—Smo—Smooo …" She had covered her face with her hands and sobbed.

Her mother had stood up, walked toward me, and proclaimed, "Look at what Professor Smolic did to my poor daughter. If nobody punishes him, I will do it!" Tears had filled her eyes. "Professor Smolic asked my daughter to come to school on Saturday to learn how to use a gun. I was suspicious, but she explained that extracurricular activities were scheduled on weekends. Mr. Smolic drove her into the woods and raped her. After that my daughter became afraid and depressed. That was when she began stuttering. We don't know what to do!" Nada's mother had cried to me.

Wiping my watery eyes, I pushed the bad memories back. The principal fixed his glasses, coughed a little bit, and continued, "The second good news is that Cyrillic is our permanent alphabet. In all of our schools we are going to use only Cyrillic, the letters of our fathers, grandfathers, and great-grandfathers. All documents, students' names, and lesson plans must be written in Cyrillic."

The German language teacher, Mrs. Stojcic, whispered, "I don't know Cyrillic."

"I'll help you. You can learn it." I gave her the quiet sign as the principal gazed at us.

"We are now masters of our own future. We have decided that we will use the Serbian dialect on a regular basis now." The principal smiled. "By the way, I have to announce that three of our colleagues: Professor Luka, Professor Sanja, and Professor Alma chose not to join us." *Why would they resign?* I asked myself. *Professor Luka has worked at the school for many years, longer than I had. His home is across the river in Croatia. He was a good sociology and philosophy teacher. Our school is the only one in the area that offers those subjects. What about professors Alma and Sanja, the two young teachers from Jajce? A Serbian radio station*

74

reported that their army brought "freedom" to that town. Were they forced to leave? Where are they now? I looked at our current team. *I am the only Muslim teacher left. How long will I be here?*

I couldn't bear to listen to the principal any longer and stared out the window. Several buses were parked on the street in front of the school. Sorrowful people were waiting to be inspected before exiting their dear country. Their only fault was that they were Muslim or Catholic. Family members, cousins, and friends were walking around the buses and wiping their faces. My eyes filled with tears too. *It is our destiny.*

Chapter 4—**Struggles**

I dream of giving birth to a child who will ask, "Mother, what was 'war'?"

–Eve Merriam

The Conundrums

All of my expectations had been wrong. I had been sure that Husein and other Muslims and Croats on the hospital staff would receive calls to return back to work soon, but our telephone remained silent. Some of Husein's colleagues left town, fleeing to other countries. Every time a car slowed or stopped in front of our house, we looked at each other scared that the Serb military police were coming for Husein. He couldn't eat well and spent many sleepless nights filling the house with the smoke of cigarettes.

It had finally come to the question that neither one of us wanted to ask: *Should the two of us, Husein and myself, for the sake of our family, separate temporarily?* Other husbands and wives had done it. Some husbands had left for Austria or Germany or Sweden, but until that moment we had not seriously considered that option for ourselves. *If we separated, when would we reunite? How would our broken family survive the war?*

We went to Mehmed and Adevija's home to seek help with our dilemma. "I am not sure that Nana is able to travel. It may be better for Husein if he goes alone and stays with one of his brothers, either the one in Austria or the one in Germany. I will pray to God to protect us," I proposed, my voice still shaking. "You, Mehmed and Adevija, are like my parents, and I know you will watch out for us. I hope the war will stop soon, and that Husein will be able to return."

"We came to ask you for advice." Husein looked at his lap. "I don't know what to do. Would I survive if the Serb army ordered me to dig trenches for them? "

"I was so happy when you bought the lot for your home on

76

our street," Adevija added. "It felt like we had expanded our family and gained more children around us. Now we are confused about your future and our own."

"This is very complicated," commented Mehmed. "I'm afraid to give you any advice. If something bad happened, I would never forgive myself. You must make that decision."

Husein took a cigarette from Mehmed's box, and soon clouds of smoke hung in the room. "Every step now could be a misstep. If I stay here, I am sure the Serbs will eventually enlist me. I have a short temper, so I would end up protesting their injustices toward other Bosnians and they would kill me." He became quiet and took a sip of coffee.

The sunlight was disappearing from the horizon, and the room was filling with evening darkness. Adevija lit a candle. "If your family leaves, the Serbs will certainly occupy your house and take all of your belongings," Adevija noted. "That injustice is what makes me think you should stay. Everything that you earned during more than twenty years of your marriage will go to your enemies. How can you allow that?"

Mehmed stood up and paced the room. He looked at Husein. "It is heartbreaking, but safety is our number one priority. Is your thirteen-year-old son safe here?" He faced me. "Who would protect you and your elderly mother-in-law? If we could spend nights together, I would agree that Husein goes. But Adevija has a lot of pain in her knees, and she cannot come to your house every night. On the other hand, Nana is in a worse condition than my wife. How could I protect you?" Mehmed then opened his empty palms.

"Nana is too old to travel," I agreed. "She can hardly walk to the bathroom in our house. I have to work, and Samir is too young for army duty. I hope with God's help we will be fine here. One day this terrible war will stop. It cannot go on forever."

Adevija looked at me and smiled. "Aisa, I admire your bravery. Is your confidence coming from our Cimirotic roots?"

"We do have some brave people in the Cimirotic family, but I rely on God," I explained. "I am going to ask Him for guidance and protection. Prayers are powerful. God is the source of all knowledge, and He knows what is best."

"Nana and Samir are frightened sitting in the dark not knowing where we are," said Husein as he stood up. I walked with him. A thick, dark cloud covered the entire town in the chilly October night, and I shivered. All of our neighborhoods' houses looked like ominous castles covered with the gloom of night.

"Are you sure you can stay in this dark place without me?" Husein asked.

"It is not going to be easy, but I am afraid for your life. I only want all of us to stay alive."

The Paycheck

At the end of the school day, my colleague Mila was waiting for me in the hallway with a bright smile. *What lies behind that smile?* I wondered as I approached her warily.

"Did your husband pick up his paycheck?" she asked.

"No, he hasn't gone to the hospital since the military police refused him entrance two months ago." I looked into her eyes.

"He has a right to his pay for the days he worked," she whispered. "By the way, I have more news to share," she added, looking around. "The entire hospital staff attended Dr. Zec's father's funeral. Dr. Tendzeri suggested calling your husband back to work, but what surprised me was that your dear friend, Dr. Dobrmilovic, opened his big mouth. He said that if Dr. Softic returned, he would resign. I couldn't keep quiet and reminded him that you had been friends, but his wife pointed out that your child is in America and safe while our kids are having nightmares here."

I remained quiet, digesting the information and searching for appropriate words. "We never know who our real friends are," I responded with a sigh. "If Husein doesn't work, Dr. Dobromilovic and his 'friends' will be able to make more money. Most people are caught up in a competition for recognition, titles, and power, and they achieve these things by putting others down or deceiving them." It was painful. Hope dies last, and I mourned the death of my hope that Husein would get his job back and be able to stay with us.

To be alone with my thoughts I took a shortcut home on the quiet streets. *Husein will never be called back to work. He must leave us as soon as possible. I'll stay. I cannot give the Serbs our house and land and reward them for their crimes. Our house is built with bricks made from my father and grandfather's clay, and I have a right to fight for it. It is my duty, my task. I'll be the winner with God's help. In His holy book, God says that the person who is a believer and does good deeds does not need to feel fear or sorrow. Staying in my home with my thirteen-year-old son and eighty-seven-year-old mother-in-law will be a test for me. I'll be thankful to God for whatever He provides for us. If He allows somebody to murder me in my home, He will reward me in the hereafter,* inshallah. *I have known many brave women who had God's support in their lives. Look at my mother—when my father died, she stayed in our house and, thank God, raised us into responsible and good human beings. Both of my grandmothers were young widows and survived with their children.*

The light-blue building is the hospital, the place where Husein worked for about twenty years. His last day there was August 8, 1992 when he worked for twenty-four hours straight.

My palms sweated, and my heart beat rapidly when I informed Husein about his last paycheck. It looked like my words had opened an unhealed wound. Husein raised his eyebrow, and his forehead wrinkled. He stood, and his footsteps disturbed the room's silence. He raised his head and lamented, "I have been home for two months, yet no one has called me. Why? I worked there for twenty years, all of my professional life. I spent my holidays there and many, many nights. If a dog stayed there all that time, somebody would think about that animal. I cannot go back asking for the money. Period." He couldn't talk for a moment. "Tomorrow I will go to the police station to ask what documents I need to visit my brother in Austria. I cannot sit here and wait for the military police to come and pick me up."

The next day Hussein went to the police station. A policeman crossed Husein's name off of the citizen registration book, cut one corner off of his ID card, and gave him a travel permit.

"Officially I am not longer Bosnian. They cannot schedule me for army duty," Husein explained, showing me his clipped ID card. With vacant eyes Husein raised his head and whispered, "I want to die. It would be best if someone broke in the house and killed me. It would finish all our problems." Husein wiped his tears.

I quietly took his wet hand. "This is the most painful and difficult decision in our lives," I offered, "but we cannot lose hope in God's mercy. We are honest and truthful people, and God will help us. This is our test, and we must deal with it."

The next day after work I walked straight to the hospital. It was almost a second home to him, and his work there was a part of who he was. The building was the same, but everything felt different—strange, somewhat frightening, and empty. It was hard to believe how much things had changed in only a few months. Even though I was walking on asphalt, it felt as if I were moving through a deep, muddy creek. I gasped for air. I was covered with a cold sweat by the time I made my way up the three flights of stairs. Noticing Dr. Borisavljevic, I walked toward him.

"Where is my colleague, Dr. Softic?" he asked with a sarcastic laugh. "I haven't heard anything about him for months. I suppose he's a successful farmer by now!" he said with a chuckle.

I couldn't answer for a moment, couldn't stand to look at the grin on his face and listen to his laughter. Finally I forced myself to look up, and my eyes narrowed as any person's would when looking at something despicable. I thought, *How can you be celebrating the misery of one of your colleagues? Do you have the ability to imagine yourself in his shoes? My husband studied medicine, not agriculture, and practiced his profession with distinction for twenty years. And now you and your friends have locked him out for no good reason. And you mock him. Wait—just wait—you don't know what life has in store for you.*

"This is not funny, nor is it time for jokes," I replied in quiet anger.

His smile disappeared, and he turned his head away.

The woman in charge of payroll approached me. "Mrs. Softic, this is the money for Dr. Softic. Please sign here," she stated, handing me a pay envelope and a form to sign. I squeezed the pen hard to prevent my hand from shaking as I signed my name. I was unable to thank her because my tears were gathering like a storm ready to burst, and I didn't want to give Dr. Borisavljevic any additional reason for enjoyment over our family's pain. With Husein's envelope in hand and my broken heart bleeding, I left the hospital.

Light in Darkness

Fahro Bradaric, a senior student in my class, was waiting in the hallway for me when I arrived at school. He came closer and whispered, "Almost every night the bus I take home to Orahova is filled with drunk, armed Serb soldiers. If they find out that I am Muslim, they might kill me. Do you have an extra room in your home that I could stay in?"

"Aida's room is empty," I replied softly. "I will talk to my husband, but I am almost sure that you can come live with us tomorrow."

"Thank you very much. Please ask Dr. Softic how much he is going to charge me."

"The room is free. I'm busy and do not cook fancy dishes, but you are welcome to eat what we have," I explained with a smile.

The next day Fahro came home with me. Leaving his suitcase in the hallway, he took a quick look at his room and explained, "I have only a few minutes to pray the evening prayer. I don't want to miss it." His diligence about observing the prayer time impressed me. Fahro led the prayer, his beautiful voice filling the room and transporting me to another peaceful world. When Fahro said, "God is greater," I was no longer afraid of rifles, bombs, soldiers, or cars pulling up in front of our home—of anything.

When we finished the evening prayer, Fahro continued to pray alone. "I made up some prayers I missed. I asked Allah to help me be diligent enough to complete all five prayers every day. If I miss one, I make it up as soon as I am able to."

He is Aida's age and prays five times every day. I looked at this young man. I knew some old people who performed all of the daily prayers on a regular basis but I had never met a young person who did so. I had always thought that religious observance was something that grew with age.

Fahro, noticing my confusion, explained, "Last year I decided to pray all five prayers and asked God to help me do so. In the beginning I struggled, but I was persistent. Now I am able to complete them almost every day, *Alhamdulillah.*" A pleasant energy beamed from his blue eyes.

Looking at this young man, Husein confided, "I prayed a lot when I was a child. At times imams would live in our house, and they taught me and the other kids how to pray. I didn't understand Arabic, so the words that I repeated I did not comprehend. As I grew up, I prayed less and less. When I became a doctor, I didn't pray at all. I had money, respect, and a family, but also persistent restlessness, as though something was missing from my life. This evening has been a grace for me, *Alhamdulillah*. It is time that I return to prayer and ask for God's forgiveness and guidance."

I analyzed my own spiritual life and found myself somewhere in between the two of them. I thought I was devout especially compared to people my age, many of whom hardly ever prayed. For years I completed some morning and evening prayers. During the midday and afternoon prayers I was at work or busy with earthly tasks. Many nights I was too tired for the night prayer—only on Thursdays was always special. The new day in Muslims' world starts after sunset and Thursday night is considered as Friday. I believe that Friday has an hour when God fulfills believers' and I wanted to be closer to God on that day.

"The devil does not want us to be close to God," Fahro explained quietly, "so he continually whispers excuses for us not to fulfill God's commands—we have no time, we are tired, we will pray later in life. Who can guarantee that we will live to be old?"

Fahro's presence in our home was a blessing. I prayed five times every day and found that my spiritual growth made me stronger and more prepared to handle the challenges that kept coming.

Ready Shoes

In November 1992, Husein decided to obtain the documents necessary to travel to Austria as a refugee. The decision devastated him. As had happened to other refugees, Husein not only had to leave his family and all of his belongings, but he also had to pay for documents showing that all of our bills were paid in full. He even had to pay for bills we never had, such as one for "public heating." This was pure robbery on the state level. Husein's mind wrestled with worry about us staying in Bosnia and with uncertainty concerning what was waiting for him in a foreign country. The skin around his eyes and mouth took on the creased look of an oak tree's bark, and his dark hair began to turn silver around his ears. He couldn't get to sleep before midnight, and many times he'd sit up in bed until dawn. Some nights he found himself wide-awake, listening to the nearby sounds of the owls.

Nana moved her prayer beads with her fingers and whispered constantly, "Dear God, protect my son. Please protect him." From time to time I noticed her facing the wall, wiping her tears with the corner of her scarf. She barely talked. I checked on her often in the middle of the night and always found her sitting up in her bed and moving her head and shoulders in the same rhythm as a baby rocks in a cradle. I was worried how she was going to deal with the separation from her son.

Samir's face was pale. He ate only a small portion of his meals, stopped smiling and singing, and walked around in silence. I tried to be an umbrella and protect everybody. I was concerned for Nana's emotions, as well as Samir's and my own, but my husband's safety took priority. I knew that I could not protect them or myself. I didn't have any weapons, and I didn't give a thought to acquiring any. I knew that only God could protect and safeguard us, and that gave me confidence.

As Husein's departure approached, Nana's restlessness increased. In the middle of November I came home from work and noticed her holding Husein's white shoes in her shaky hands. She looked at the shoes and said, "I will go too. Only Allah knows how much I hate to go, but I don't want to keep you and this child here

85

because of me. Samir is like a pearl. Every day I thank Allah for such a kind, considerate, and wise child. I am eighty-seven years old, ready to give my soul to God any minute, but still He keeps me here for His reasons." She shifted the shoes into one hand and wiped her tears with the other.

I looked at her shaking body and couldn't keep my own tears at bay. I put a hand on her fragile shoulder and helped her sit down. I was still puzzled about the shoes.

"I am always cold. My feet are like ice, and I cannot walk without wool socks. I am going to travel in my wool socks and in Hussein's shoes. I tried all of them, and these fit the best. They are not heavy, and I am able to walk around the entire room as long as I hold onto the wall," explained Nana as she began crying again. Through her tears she prayed, "Oh dear God, our enemies destroyed our peace. Help us to recover, and give them what they deserve."

I handed Nana her cup of hot coffee and looked at her wrinkled face and red eyes.

I was deeply touched with her decision to travel. "Nana, let Husein go alone now. If it gets worse, we will join him. The shoes are ready." Nana took a sip of the coffee, and her face became brighter.

Hussein came from another room, looked at his shoes and his old mother, and tears formed and rolled down his face as well. In a shaking voice he declared, "Separation is heartbreaking, worse than death. Who can say when or if we will ever meet again?" All three of us sobbed. Separation—our most wrenching test—was upon us.

Monday, November 20, 1992, the day of Husein's departure, was like a funeral. Husein's sisters, neighbors, and friends filled the house early in the morning. I served cake and juice, but many of our visitors hardly touched it. I hid my gaze from my sister, Dervisha, and my sister-in-law, Satka, to keep myself from crying loudly. I was emotionally exhausted and ready to collapse.

Our guests were quiet. Nana whispered her prayers. I wanted to protect Samir from the situation. I found his book bag and reminded him to go to school. When I saw tears in his eyes and Husein's hand on his shoulder, I set the bag down and became quiet. Samir said that he planned to follow his father as far as the Sava River and wave to him on its shore. All of the people in the room sobbed. I glanced at Nana to be sure that she was able to control her emotions.

When I heard the voice of the driver, Nail, my hands became shaky. I asked my neighbor Esma to serve coffee and ran to the bathroom on the second floor. I took a towel, squeezed it in my hands, covered my face, and cried. My whole body was shaking uncontrollably. After a few minutes, cold water chilled my face, and the pressure in my head and chest subsided. I whispered, "Dear God, this is too hard for me. Improve my strength and help me carry my load properly."

All the guests downstairs were standing except Nana. She was still sitting, looking at her lap, and moving her prayer beads. Husein came closer to her, knelt by her sofa, and hugged her tightly. She let the beads go and placed both of her hands around his neck. Husein kissed her wet cheeks and sobbed. Everyone cried. Nail took Hussein's suitcases and walked toward his car. Hussein hugged each person in turn before he walked out with all of us following like mourners behind him. When Husein reached the car, he opened its door and then raised his eyes to the house. He paused a moment and ran up the steps and back inside.

I assumed that he had forgotten something and followed him. He opened the door to Nana's room. He walked over to her, took her in his arms, and held her in a tender embrace, as though he knew that this was their final good-bye, the last time they would lay eyes on each other in this world.

"I am all right, my son," she assured him. "This is Allah's plan, and we must follow it. We all belong to Allah, and we have to return to Him. May Allah bless you and protect you."

Husein sat next to her, placed his hand on her shoulder, and wiped his tears.

"Go, my son," Nana asserted as she gently removed his hand from her shoulder. "They are waiting for you. I believe we will meet in another, better world."

Husein squeezed his mother. The bitterness of their parting touched their faces, and tears spoke for them. He walked straight to the car, opened the door and sat down. I looked at him. He placed his elbows on his knees, looked at his lap, and held his head in his hands. The car moved slowly away with Samir running behind it. The people who had seen us through our parting slowly left, one by one, until I stood alone beside the street, tearless now, looking into the distance where the car had disappeared.

The street where I said goodbye to Husein

Lonely Life

After Husein's departure, our house and hearts felt empty. Husein's sisters came often to visit their mother, but things were not the same. Nura, Husein's youngest and favorite sister, uttered, "It is hard to keep my head up when everything around us is falling down."

"The happiest day in my life was when my brother came home with his medical degree," Hata, the oldest sister, shared, pausing for a moment, "and look at all of us now."

Shuhra, picked a cup of cold coffee and added, "He has had a tough life. He left home in the sixth grade for the town of Dubica to finish his elementary school. Later, he traveled to Gradiska from Orahova for high school. He stayed with me during his junior year, the year I had my twins. We were very poor. We didn't even have a cow until Husein asked our father to give us one. During his last year in high school, Husein stayed in Tuzla with our sister Hadera. After that came medical school, residency, a family, a house. And now, when he is at the age where he can begin to slow down and take things easier, he loses everything."

Nana raised her head and asserted emphatically, "Our deeds go with us. God said that on the Judgment Day everyone's deeds, both good and bad, will be revealed. I hope God will reward him for his tough path in seeking knowledge. What is this world in comparison to the hereafter?" Nana's comments opened our eyes, reminded us of our faith, and filled our hearts with hope.

In the late afternoon Samir came back home and announced, "I hugged father before he climbed into the car at the border. I walked to the shore of the Sava River and waved until the car disappeared over the bridge."

Without Husein, the house seemed to close in around me. I walked over to an open window to get a breath of fresh air. The sun, a golden ball, was sinking in the west. A couple of buses and hundreds of cars moved slowly along Mine Street, a river of refugees. *All of those people like their town, their river, their gardens and their homes, but fear for own life made them leave. I am afraid for my life too.* Suddenly, I wished to be in that stream with my son, mother-in-law, and with Husein. I walked between the door and the window like hungry mouse in a labyrinth. *I made mistake. We must go. It is impossible to obtain the necessary documents now.* The room spun, and I leaned back against the cold wall, exhausted, my soul in pain and every muscle and joint aching. I collapsed like a wet rag on the sofa.

Nana stood up and offered, "Life is rough sometimes and does not always go in the direction that we want it to. You must be strong. You are the foundation of this family."

Samir's lemonade and my coffee relieved my headache a bit, and I sat up. My tears dulled the ache in my soul, and I wanted more than ever to share my feelings with Husein. *Why couldn't we make a better decision? Why didn't we leave together? I'm hurt. I am weak, unable to take care of myself. Who will take care of Nana and Samir? We'll join you as soon as possible.* It was midnight, but I couldn't close my burning eyes.

Now that Husein had left, Samir behaved as the man of the house. At first darkness, he pulled the blinds down and boarded the door for extra protection. I lit a candle and served supper. We gathered around the brightness and fresh food like three orphans. The light played on our faces, but our souls were empty. Our happiness died. Each of us missed Husein in a different way. Nana missed her son—her support and her comfort. Samir missed his father—his security and protection. And I missed my husband—my best friend.

One night Samir was finishing his homework and forgot to pull down the blinds. A huge fire in our neighborhood brightened the room. I peered through the window at the burning house. As the fire progressed, I became frightened, asking, "Samir, look at this fire. How many houses are burning?"

He jumped and pulled the blinds down. "Come away from the window. It's just children playing–I'm sure that they made the fire. Don't worry. Come here and read a book." Samir behaved as my parent, and suddenly I became the child that he wanted to protect from danger. I sighed, worried that the huge burden could overwhelm him.

Husein arrived safely in Austria. I called him on his brother's telephone, and we talked for a few minutes on a weekly basis. He had one long, narrow room furnished with a bed, an iron dresser, and a small hot plate. He shared a bathroom and a shower room with the other refugees. He kept his suitcases under his bed. For the first several weeks he sounded all right, and I was calm.

My Last Teaching Day

In the middle of December 1992, I sensed trouble. A series of strange dreams alerted me to danger. In one of them, several huge snakes tried to catch me and sink their teeth into my arms and legs. In another, I went to school dressed in a traditional Muslim outfit and wasn't allowed to enter the classroom.

This is the school where I worked from 1977 to 1992. I served as principal from 1988 to 1991.
My time at the school ended abruptly in December 1992.

The last day before winter break, as I entered the school where I had been a teacher and then principal for 15 years, I learned the meaning of my dreams. Murisa Kozarcanin, a custodian and my dear friend, waited for me. Her look of worry grubbed my attention.

"Aisa, I have important news for you," Murisa whispered. "Today is your last day here. It's also the last day for Belkisa Harbas, Mirsada Lovic, Hikmeta, and me." She swallowed hard. "This morning Principal Lazarevic, wrote on the board in the teachers' break room: 'Anyone who does not have a husband, son, or brother in the Serb army cannot keep their job at this school anymore.'" She lowered her voice just above whispering. "But it is worse than that." She stepped closer. "When I brought coffee to the break room, I heard a group of teachers mentioning your name. I acted like I was cleaning a table so I could hear what was going on. Mr. Smolic asked why you were still teaching here. He said that if nobody kicked you out of the school, he would do so with his rifle. Yes, he said, 'with his rifle.' I heard it with my own ears." Murisa's eyes communicated the fear that had taken hold of her. She looked from hallway to hallway, and her hands trembled to all the sounds around us.

"I'm scared for you," Murisa continued. "I know that you live with your teenage son and your old mother-in-law. You don't have any protection or any source of strength to lean on."

I was speechless for a while. "Thank you, Murisa, but don't worry about me. I'll be fine." My words mixed with the sounds of her steps as she walked down the hall. I couldn't move.

Silence accompanied me and I prayed, *Dear God, I know that all of our life is Your test. Please guide me to pass it and to earn Your satisfaction. What can I do without a job? How can my son, my mother-in-law, and I live without any money? Dear Lord, accept my prayers, help me find a good path, and help us survive. Amen.*

I stood up and walked slowly toward the teachers' break room. My hands were suddenly ice cold, so I held my purse tightly to steady their shaking. I entered the room, greeted the people there, and took my regular place close to the door. The room was full and eerily silent. My colleagues were avoiding my eyes, unwilling to meet my gaze. *Are they afraid of me or of their consciences?* I asked myself. *Why change now? We worked together for fifteen years. Is it a sin to be a Muslim? Where are my friends now?*

The bell broke the silence. I raised my head in the empty room, grabbed my students' grade book, and walked towards the board. The sentence was there. Even though I already knew every word, I read it again. The tension built inside me. I sat down, trying to wish the sentence away as if it were a bad dream, but the words "cannot keep their job at this school anymore" were flashing in my mind. *It is true,* I thought. *Today is my last day of teaching. What should I do? Should I go to the classroom and teach my students? Can I teach them today? Should I find the principal and talk to him? Is there anybody who will help me? Anybody?*

I stood up, sighed, and headed to the classroom. The steady beats of my heart drummed in my ears. I entered the classroom, scared to observe my unusually quiet students. I stared at the topic sentence I had written, but it blurred in my mind with that fateful sentence on the board in the teachers' room. I looked at my students, hoping that their bright eyes would inspire me and give me the strength to lead the class as I had for the entire twenty-three years of

93

my teaching career. For the first time I was speechless. All twenty-five pairs of eyes of my senior students looked at me, puzzled. I loved those eyes, but I couldn't stand their confused gaze. I turned to the board to concentrate on the topic. My swollen eyes blinked several times to protect tears from coming out. Finally, I created a sentence in my mind and faced the students. Instead of words a volcano of sadness erupted, and I couldn't stop the hot flow of tears. I covered my face and fled into the hallway. I sat on the bench, supported my head with my hands, and sobbed uncontrollably.

Two students came and sat down. One of them said softly, "Mrs. Softic, what happened? How can we help you?"

"Today is my last day here," I stated, calming my wobbly voice.

"We want to help any way we can," the other student said.

"Your support and understanding is helping me enough," I replied, looking at their sad eyes.

After a few minutes I wiped my face, and walked back into the room.

"I'm sorry. I tried not to show my emotion, but it is very hard for me today. I love teaching, I love having you as students, and I love being in this school," I shared, and my voice became shaky again. I waited for a minute and explained the sentence on the board in the teachers' break room and its meaning for my life.

The classroom became a huge beehive. Several students raised their hands.

"Mrs. Softic, we should go to the military building and protest there," suggested Babic.

"We are going to protest in front of the school! We are not coming back to the school without you, Mrs. Softic," asserted Nikolic.

"Yes, yes!" the whole classroom echoed.

"Thank you, but I don't want any protests. I want you to continue your education. Knowledge is wealth that nobody can take from you. You are seniors, and the college entrance exam is ahead of you. I wish you success in your personal and professional lives," I told them from the bottom of my heart. The bell rang ending the class, and I pick up my things and walked to the door. I heard my students' sad whispers as I left the classroom, but I couldn't look back and take the chance that I would break down again.

Outside, a few yards from the school, thousands of Bosnian refugees were twisting along the Brotherhood and Unity Bridge that connected Bosnia and Croatia. The line looked like the largest and ugliest snake on Earth. Older people were standing on the Bosnian shore of the river, waving with one sad hand and drying tears with the other. Some of them were calling out in shaking voices their grandchildren's names, "Hassan, Hussein, Fatima, Amra, Leila, Said, Yusuf, Ibrahim—don't forget Nana, don't forget Grandpa, and don't forget Bosnia!" The wind muffled the grandparents' words into silence and dropped them in the river's waves.

The Bridge of Unity and Brotherhood that connects Bosnia and Croatia. The war changed life around the bridge.

As I entered my home, I spoke hesitantly, "They kicked me out of school."

"I knew it," uttered Nana. "If they could kick Husein out of the hospital, then they would surely kick you out of your school as well."

I closed my eyes and let my tears shower my face. The sobbing of all three of us filled the room. Even the candle cried with us with its melting tears.

A few hours after midnight, with no family members or friends reachable by phone, I contemplated how God made my education possible in His own mysterious way. I prayed, *Dear God, when my situation looked gloomy and dark, You sent Your light to show me the right path. You helped me to reach all of my goals. Thank You for Your vast help from the bottom of my heart.*

The Irony of the List

The winter nights—cold, dark, and filled with fear—seemed endless. We quickly ran out of candles and, like many of our neighbors, created a new source of light by burning cotton fabric strips soaked in vegetable oil. This new light source produced clouds of smoke worse than the dense cloud of cigarette smoke in a crowded café. Nana, Samir, and I gathered around it and shared our life stories to distract us from the fear of artillery or the sound of human steps. Once the rhythm of Samir's breathing assured us that he was asleep, Nana and I would pray. We knew we had no refuge other than with God, so we asked for His mercy, for the easing of our loneliness, and for His protection with so much intensity that tears accompanied our words. We would chant: "*La ilaha ilalah, La ilaha ilalah, La ilaha ilalah* (There is no god, but one God)" until we fell asleep.

One night, as I closed my tired, worried eyes, the squeaking sound of footsteps on the wooden floor froze the blood in my veins. I didn't know if a soldier or a burglar walked through the darkness a few meters from me. I panicked and tried to wake Nana up. When I touched her empty bed, I realized she must have been pacing in the dark room. My twitching nerves didn't allow me to close my eyes the rest of the night.

The next morning I dressed warmly, placed the last of my money in my pocket, took my bicycle, and headed towards the pharmacy to buy sleeping pills for Nana and me. The cold north wind urged me to push the pedals faster. When I reached downtown, I recognized Mirsada, a worker from our school, running toward me.

"You cannot imagine what our school is doing with the bonus pay from this past school year. Five names missing from the list of who is getting paid—no paychecks for the Muslims." Her voice was filled with disappointment, and her eyes burned with wrath.

In our system there was a certain amount of money allotted to the school. In December, if there was a surplus, it was to be distributed as a bonus to employees based on how many days each had worked during that fiscal year. Since I had worked every day in 1992, I should have been allotted my share.

"Wait! They must give us our part! We worked the entire year!" I raised my voice. "I have to see for myself. Do you want to go with me?"

"I cannot. I am not sure that I'll be able to control my temper." She shook her head.

I grabbed my bicycle and headed straight to the school. My blood rushed through my veins, and I didn't feel cold anymore. I carried my bicycle inside and parked it under the steps. Several teachers were waiting in line in front of the accountant's office. I joined them and felt my heart thumping in anger and apprehension as I stood waiting. When I finally reached the head of the line, the accountant, Mrs. Draganovic, told me, "I'm sorry, your name is not on the list. You need to talk to the principal. It is not my say."

"Is everybody who worked this calendar year on the list?" I asked politely, looking at all the people around me. Some of them looked at the floor, some looked through the window, and a few of them even looked at me but didn't speak. I didn't move. I wanted them to witness discrimination and injustice.

Mrs. Draganovic sighed and said carefully, "I cannot make any changes. Go talk to the principal, please." I noticed fear in her brown eyes.

I left the line and walked toward the principal's office, remembering all the injustices he did toward me. *I have to talk to him… fine. I am not afraid. I only fear God.*

As I entered his office and walked toward his desk, his smile faded. He fixed his glasses and nervously straightened a pile of papers in front of him.

"Why isn't my name on the list for the bonus pay?" Rage beamed from my eyes, but I controlled my voice.

He was still looking at the papers in front of him as if the answer has been written somewhere on them. Finally he raised his head and said, "Oh, are you inquiring about that little money?" He paused. "It is a gift for people who celebrate Christmas. We all know that Christmas isn't your holiday, and therefore, you don't qualify for it." His lips moved into a horrible smile.

"Celebrating holidays has nothing to do with it. What you did is discrimination!"

As I pronounced the last word, raising my voice a bit, the principal stood, put his glasses down, narrowed his eyes, and shouted, "How dare you say such things! Are you questioning the holiday bonuses of honest, hardworking teachers? You are the most ungrateful person!" He was yelling at this point, his face turning fiery red.

"I am not questioning Christmas. You know that very well. I am simply asking why I wasn't paid what is lawfully mine," I stated in a firm voice.

He was quiet for a moment, lowered his voice, and responded, "I have an idea. Don't worry. I will give you the special increase for your holiday. 'Eid' it's called, right? I will make a request for a large permanent increase in your salary for the rest of your life. I'll make an exception, only for you, so I can correct my discrimination. Are you satisfied?" He chuckled.

My eyes barely held back my tears of anger. I couldn't talk, but I prayed silently, *Dear God, he is making fun of me. Obviously, he isn't going to do anything about the pay. I am giving our disagreement to You; You are the best judge. Please give me the ability to control myself and be patient.*

On my way home rain showered my face, and I felt that the sky cried with me. As the rain intensified, I took my scarf, covered my head and remembered the rainy, cold Tuesday in October of 1968—

*   *   *

Even with my umbrella my school uniform was soaked by the time I arrived in my school. At the end of the last class of the day I glanced through the classroom window and saw the gray sky still pouring down heavy rain. I dreaded having to return home and get wet all over again. When the bell announced the end of class, the professor opened the door. There stood my mom, drenched. Her wet scarf dripped water on her dark gray coat. Heavy with water, the coat bent my mother's shoulders.

"Mom, what are you doing here? You are all wet. Where is your umbrella?" I looked at my mom in embarrassment and did not introduce her to any of my friends. I did not want them to see her in her wet, worn villager's clothes. The two of us waited at the corner of the hallway and then walked slowly.

"I do not have an umbrella. When Alija, our horse Rous, and I left our house, it was a dry, peaceful night. It started to rain after midnight, and by that time we were more than halfway here. I was not sure whether we should return home or continue. But my wish to see and help you was stronger than the rain."

"Oh Mom, I am sorry. Are you cold?"

It looked like Mom didn't recognize my words from the slushy sound that her water-soaked rubber shoes made, rubbing against her bare feet. The empty hallway absorbed some of our sound, and water marked our path as we walked toward the school exit. Mother told me that they came to sell some of their vegetables and make money for me, but only a few people came to the flea market in that weather. She promised to try other flea markets and maybe get more money later. She opened her pocket and handed me a wet handkerchief with the money inside.

I looked at her. In her soaked clothes Mom looked even shorter. Dark circles under her eyes told me how tired she was.

Outside the rain continued to pour, but we still walked.

"Mom, take my umbrella, please. You have a long way to go."

"We are already soaked through to the skin, so an umbrella will do us no good."

I reproached myself that I had felt ashamed for my dear mother's appearance, that I had asked for money, and that I had made so much trouble for her and my brother. I was afraid that this trip would give Mom a terrible headache or back pain, and I was worried for my brother's health as well. My mouth was dry, and I couldn't talk for a while.

"Please, do not go to the Jajce flea market. I can borrow books, so I won't need money. Mom, do you hear me? I do not need money. I need you and my brother healthy. Please, do not try to make any money for me, please." I cried.

I hugged Mom and kissed her wet, cold face and noticed a gentle light in her eyes. "Oh dear Mom, our troubles will last for only a few more months. When I graduate, our problems will disappear forever. I will buy many nice clothes and a few umbrellas for you. "

Mom walked in the opposite direction from me. I rode my bike and did not open my umbrella. My throat became tight. The rain and my tears wet my face and clothes. I thought about my mom and brother in the wagon slowly making their way home behind their exhausted, wet horse.

*   *   *

The memories of all the sacrifices made for my education twenty-three years ago broke my heart, and I suddenly found myself standing like a rain-drenched statue in my street.

I was brought back to the present with a jolt as I heard and saw a tank with the Serb flag approaching. Trembling with fright I gathered my strength, ran to my neighbor's yard, and hid behind their house. My bulging eyes followed the tank's movement, and I could feel the land shake under the heavy machine. When the street became quiet again, I walked home.

Samir met me outside the house and asked, "Mom, what happened to the bicycle?"

"Bicycle? I didn't have the bicycle today. I walked home from school." I was confused why he was asking me about the bicycle.

"This morning you rode off on the bicycle," said Samir softly.

"Bicycle, bicycle ... Oh! You are right. I went to the school to get my money, but I have no money and now no bicycle. I have to walk back and get it. Hopefully it is still there."

"Mom, you worry too much these days. Please let me go and get it." Samir touched my hand. I protested, but Samir was on his way up the street before I finished my objection.

As I walked inside the house, the sound of Nana's sleeping made me smile. I had discovered the irony of the list and had even lost my bicycle. But everything happened for a reason.

5 Chapter —Strength

My past has not defined me, destroyed me, deterred me, or
defeated me; it has only strengthened me.
—Steve Maraboli

Merhamet

I sat close to a window, watching the steady rain mixed with the sounds of weapons. Everything looked dark gray. Our family was broken, as was my country. The war had brought fear and tragedy. I had no job, no income, and not even any candles. I called my dear friend and neighbor Mina to share my troubles.

"Do you know that out town has a good humanitarian agency named Merhamet? Volunteers from there are helping our people who lost jobs. Why don't you go there and get free medicine?" she asked.

I headed there right away. Mehmed Biscevic, the head of Merhamet, greeted me warmly and said that the nurse was absent. As I turned to go home, he asked me, "Mrs. Softic, are you still teaching at the high school?"

"I lost my job a week ago," I shared, disappointedly.

"What are you doing now?" he asked smiling.

I couldn't figure out why he was happy, and it took me a few seconds to open my mouth. "I am taking care of my son and my mother-in-law at home." My head was dropping in humiliation.

"One of our workers is moving to Croatia, and we have an open position here."

My eyes popped wide open. I couldn't believe what I had just heard.

"Are you offering me a job?" I asked with amazement as if I were dreaming. My eyes sparkled with excitement and relief. My heart felt like it wanted to jump out of my chest with happiness.

He nodded. "It will be our pleasure to have you with us to serve our people and help them survive these difficult days." He paused. "We don't have money and don't pay salaries, but we do share food, detergent, clothes, and anything else that we might have. I'm sure that it will help you and your family get by." He smiled.

"I would gladly work for Merhamet," I replied. "When do you want me to start?"

"Let me see." He counted the days on his fingers. "It looks like January 20."

"Is there anything else we could help you with?" He pointed at a box of powdered milk and a box of soybeans.

"Do you have any candles?" I asked sheepishly.

He walked to a shelf and picked up a handful of candles. I put them in my purse, thanking Mr. Biscevic. As I closed the door behind me, I noticed that my hands were shaking with excitement. The fresh, cold air made me feel as if I were soaring. I was standing only a few meters farther from the spot where I had met my loyal friend Mirsada earlier in the day when my optimism had been kilometers away. Even the weather had changed. The rain stopped, and the sun was shining brilliantly. *Dear God, I am not able to thank You enough. You are lifting me from my darkness to Your light. I received two pleasant surprises in one day: I have a job at Merhamet, and candles in my purse. I remember my mother asking You to bless me with unexpected blessings, and You fulfilled her wishes today.*

Merhamet was to us Muslims, like a beehive to bees—it was a meeting place and a community center, dispensing food, aid, and support to Muslims. Mina Biscevic helped people find their letters, packages, and basic items like flour, oil, sugar, and salt. When she left, Emira Kasumovic took her place. Muhamed Mehic worked with the volunteers in our town and in the villages. He counted how much basic food items the unemployed citizens could get. Some of our citizens came to Merhamet for advice or to share their fears and frustrations. Ejub and Mehmed Biscevic traveled to Zagreb to bring humanitarian aid. Muhamed Bischevic worked tirelessly in the storage room. Dr. Ines Todic and the nurse, Osman Becic, took care of the medicine. They checked, sorted, and distributed all of the donated medications. My role was to care for the children and elderly.

Nana had enough sleep medicine, but every four days or so she would have to take a different kind depending on what had been donated to Merhamet. One night she took a sleeping pill right before dinner and fell asleep before she even finished eating. Samir and I called her, moved her hands, shook her shoulders, but we couldn't wake her. I placed a pillow under her head and tugged the bed sheet under her arms, but she remained sleeping.

I ran outside to see if I could call for help to take her to the emergency room. There was no light anywhere. The wind silently moved the pine tree branches, and a distant machine gun disturbed the silence. I came back to the room and sat close to Nana.

"This medicine is too strong for Nana," I said, holding her small hand, wrinkled with age and creased with work.

"What did she take?" Samir asked.

"I brought four new pills today."

"Did she take all of them?" Samir glanced at her with fear in his eyes.

"She always takes one pill before supper." I replied, searching for the rest of her medicine. I found the three pills in their original packs wrapped tightly in the corner of her scarf. Samir quickly brought a candle closer, and we tried to read the description and side effects, but we couldn't understand the language. I crushed the medicine and threw it in the garbage.

Many Muslims came to Merhamet to share their sadness and memories of our nine mosques, which were destroyed in Bosanska Gradiska, Orahova, Dubrave, Liskovac, Obradovac, Rovine, and Catrnja from November 11, 1992 to April 11, 1993. A huge part of our hearts went with them. Even though some of the mosques were kilometers away the explosions were so strong that my house shook in response to the impact. A million pieces of brick, wood, cement, stone, and glass covered the cemetery surrounding the mosques. Some of the graves, gravestones, and nearby Muslim houses were damaged too. Several uprooted trees lay on top of the graves as if hugging them. Our hearts ached at the realization that even our dead couldn't rest in peace.

I liked our mosques. I began to attend religious lessons in my village mosque when I was a first grader. My world was there. The peaceful building where I had found profound tranquility was on one side of the road, and the graves of my father, uncle, grandmother, cousins, and neighbors were on the other. I would stand in front of the white gravestones and ask God to forgive the sins of the deceased. My first religious performance in front of hundreds of villagers was in the mosque. There I learned how to pray to God, and how to respect and love people.

From November 1992 to April 1993 all nine mosques were destroyed. After the war all the mosques were rebuilt on the same sites.

In my adult life, even though I believed in God, I seldom attended the mosques. I was a teacher, and in the Yugoslavia of that time, it would not be acceptable to see an educator in a mosque. Socialism was a government establishment, and it preached atheism. It would be grounds for disqualification if a teacher, a holder of a government position, openly proclaimed a belief in God. Our mosques were almost empty. It was only on Fridays and during the month of Ramadan that small crowds would gather there. It was not God whom we tried to please but those who held powerful positions. We did not follow the examples of the messengers Abraham, Moses, Jesus, and Muhammad—peace be upon them. Our mosques may have been demolished as a wakeup call.

A young woman who had entered the office interrupted my reflections. "Don't worry, God is forgiving and merciful. With God's will we will build new, bigger, and brighter mosques. Every minaret top landed upright, just as it was originally placed. Our wise old villagers tell us that means another mosque will be built on the same site."

"You speak great words. It is very good news," I responded with calmness in my voice.

"People cannot destroy the mosques we have within us. Every time we mention Allah's name, ask His forgiveness, and thank Him, it is like we are in a mosque."

I smiled a little remembering how young Samir's heart clung to the mosque like a magnet to metal. The wet footprints throughout the house were evidence that Samir had performed ablutions before he went there for prayer. The imam had made a key for him, so in case he was absent, Samir could still enter the mosque and pray.

My sadness lessened as I heard a vigorous man's voice, "Our strength is our trust in God. These days are good days to purify our hearts and rid ourselves of our arrogance by helping other people and telling them the good news of God's forgiveness, wisdom, knowledge, and mercy. Yes, tell them about God's attributes." An elderly man nodded in response.

"When our hearts become pure enough and when peace comes, we will build new and better houses of God, *inshallah*," explained a neighbor, Adam looking at us with sparkling eyes.

I grew spiritually during the two years I worked in Merhamet, where I witnessed the personal tragedies of the war, listened to people's stories, and cried with them as they grieved their losses.

In the beginning of 1993, a young lady, tall and shy, came to our office. Her silk scarf was mirrored in her beautiful blue eyes, making them flash like the sea on a sunny day. Nervously playing with her purse, she told me, "I am going to Banja Luka to visit my brother Ahmed. His lawyer has urged him to leave Bosnia and go to another country just as soon as he is released from jail, and I intend to go with him."

As Mr. Bishcevic asked how her brother was doing, she replied, "Ahmed is patient." Returning our gaze, she continued, "You probably know what happened six months ago." She sighed. "We decided to stay in our house in Liscovac, and my brother bought a pistol. He placed it under his pillow. One late night several burglars in military uniforms broke the glass in our door and a window and entered our house. They broke everything that they touched, shouting, 'Where are you, *balija*? Why didn't you leave yet? What are you waiting for? It looks like you will go underground.'" She cleared her throat. "Finally, Ahmed grabbed his pistol and fired it, wounding one of the intruders. They screamed and ran, dragging the wounded man out of the house. My brother called the military and civil police to explain what had happened. The police tortured my brother and put him in jail." She rose in her chair and wiped her face. "I am thankful to Allah that truth prevailed. The lawyer was able to successfully defend my brother on the grounds that he shot in self-defense as a last resort."

"I hope Allah will make it easy for you to obtain travel documents and find a better place for you and your brother," I said and hugged her. Mr. Bishcevic filled her bag with food for her brother. Her eyes shone with gratitude.

A few minutes later, Merhamet's neighbor Nijaz Galic entered, moving an empty plastic bag back and forth from one hand to another and blinking back tears. He said, "I can't believe what happened."

I gave him a chair. He sat, dropped his head, and sighed deeply. We all gathered around him. He explained, "I heard that Radnik, the company where I worked for thirty years, was distributing flour to its retired people. I grabbed this bag and went there. A security guard at the entrance door let me come in, and I followed the signs and found people distributing flour. When it was my turn, I opened my bag and waited for the young worker to give me my portion. He smiled to my face and asked where my son was. It seemed strange, but I told him that my son had gone to Denmark. He didn't move. I repeated it assuming that he didn't hear me. He cursed and screamed furiously at me, grabbed me by my shirtfront, and kicked me out with all of his strength. I rolled down the street like a large snowball down a hill. Thank God I didn't break any of my old bones." He revealed his bloody elbows and knees as he wiped away his tears.

"Don't cry. We have flour for you," I assured him.

"I am not crying for flour. I am crying about how that young man treated me. I built that factory! We were the first workers there and started in one small building. We made furniture for four hours a day and built that huge building for the other four hours. I was proud, as if I were building my own house. In the new building I worked for thirty years until I retired. That young 'donkey' treated me worse than a dog. How dare he?" Nijaz put his wrinkled hands on his face and cried like a child.

"I am sorry," said Nurse Osman as he cleaned Nijaz's wounds.

I put my hand on his trembling shoulder, telling him, "Mr. Nijaz, you know better than I that Almighty God will give that young man what he deserves. Don't worry. God is the best judge."

"You are right," responded Nijaz in a calmer voice. "My children are abroad and my wife died. I came here to share my sadness. You are my new family."

Nijaz stood up, moved slowly through the room, opened the door, and walked downstairs. The light drafts played with his gray hair as he made his way down the steps and away from the building.

Almost every morning in Merhamet we heard sad news about the torturing and killing of Muslims. An elderly couple, Mr. Ramo Shabanagic and his wife Fehima, were killed and burned in their house, a few hundred meters from Merhamet. Mr. Izudin Deronjic was wrapped in duct tape and smothered in his house. Mr. and Mrs. Zahirovic were stabbed to death. Serbs killed Mr. and Mrs. Salihbashic in their house and beat their son who died after seven days in the hospital in Banja Luka. Tevhida Beganovic, a young Muslim lady from a suburban area, was killed when soldiers broke

106

into her home. Her husband was faster, jumping out of the window to escape. Serb soldiers didn't wait until night to kill people. Halid Hasanbegovic and his wife Mina were killed in their home on the morning of February 25, 1993.

Life Crushed

In December 1993, in the late night hours, several Muslim houses were destroyed. On the Serb local news the next day it was reported that Muslims were blowing up their own homes to attract international attention. Osman, the nurse at Merhamet, came to work, shook his head, looked at the radio with an angry gaze, and told us, "We had a terrible night. My mother-in-law, Djehva, is homeless now." He paced through the room as he spoke. "Her house was on Voislav Cicic Street. After sunset, as she pulled the blinds down and prayed her evening prayer, she heard cars driving away from her house. As the night grew on, she became anxious and worried that something was going on around her house. She peeked through a window, and the street and neighboring Serb houses looked empty. She put all of her documents in her purse, packed a single suitcase with her clothes, grabbed her coat, and ran to our house. There was no way that we could sleep. Sometime after midnight we heard a loud explosion. She knew that it was her home that had been blown up."

Osman couldn't talk. He wiped his tears. There was no such thing as homeowner's insurance. Homes were self-built, one room at a time over several years. If a home was destroyed, its inhabitants were homeless.

I picked up the phone and called Osman's home. Djehva answered, "This morning I walked to the place where I had lived for more than half a century. When I arrived, all that was left was a ruin—a pile of bricks, concrete, wood, glass, and smashed furniture. This rubble is my new reality. More than fifty years of living has been replaced by a memory of what once was. All my life is now crushed. My heart aches." She paused, and I waited quietly for her to continue. After a time she cleared her throat, saying, "Suddenly, a policeman came to my pile. He had a notebook and a pen in his hands. He climbed to the top of the pile and looked at all the neighboring houses. The happiness in his eyes and a noticeable smile on his lips pierced my heart. I picked up one brick with the thought that I wanted to wipe out his happiness. He sensed danger, touched his pistol, and looked at me. The muscles in my hand became weak, and the brick slid down. I raised both hands in front of my chest and prayed loudly: 'Dear God, I am asking You by Your Mercy, Your

Majesty, Your Power, Your Strength, and all of Your other attributes, to punish the person who destroyed my home last night. Smash his life as he smashed my home. Make his heart ache like my heart is aching now. Almighty, stone his body, so he cannot do this to anybody again. I know You are hearing me.' The policeman shouted at me to be quiet, cursed, kicked bricks, and left my place mumbling."

The next night a loud explosion after midnight woke me up. Remembering Djehva's story, I walked across the room for a few minutes, peeked through a window, and stood behind a curtain in silence so still that I could hear my heart beating like a drum in my ears. I stood there in the darkness and waited for the next explosion. My nerves twitched as I attempted to assess the distance of the explosion from my house, terrified that I might possibly be blown up in the next instant. I shut my drained eyes for a couple of seconds, and the pictures of Djehva's ruined home chilled my skin. I heard shots—one, two, and three.

I shivered and ran to Nana's room. *Should I awake Samir and Nana and tell them to run? Nana could hardly walk. It is January and freezing. So where could we go?* I sat close to Nana's feet and covered myself with her warm blanket. The fearful night was still, and it seemed as if it would never pass.

Finally, dawn's light touched my sleepless eyes. It was time to go to work. On my way I noticed a partially destroyed house only three blocks from Merhamet. Looking through a hole that had once been a window, the bloody walls were visible. Bricks, smashed furniture, clothes, and toys were scattered in the yard.

I joined the crowd of about twenty or twenty-five people. A short, elderly man, angry as a raging fire, was walking up and down the street shouting, "O my dear son and my daughter-in-law, Serbs killed you. Yes, your own people killed you! Shame on them! God, look what they did to my children and what they did to our poor Muslim neighbors." He sat in the yard, covered his face, and sobbed for a while. Suddenly, he stood up and raised his hands. "Serbs can come to kill me too. I don't care. I am not afraid of them." He looked at the bloody toys and lamented, "Oh, my two poor orphans, Serbs killed your father and your mother. Remember it! Yes, Serbs did it!"

I recognized several of our neighbors in the crowd, and we exchanged confused glances.

As I entered Merhamet, my co-worker, Sanela, swooped down the steps and whispered, "Two young Serbs were killed in the house explosion. The father of the young man is furious. We can hear how he blames Serbs for his family's tragedy."

Just as I opened my mouth to describe my own fearful night, Mr. Bishcevic entered, shouting, "Lock the door! Lock the door! Something terrible happened! It was terrible!"

His words put a hollow feeling in the pit of my stomach. I locked the door, and all four of us gathered around him. He sat on a chair, held his head with one hand, and wiped his forehead with a handkerchief from the other. He became silent.

"What happened?" Osman asked nervously.

Instead of answering, he leaned his head back against the wall and closed his eyes. His black eyebrows and the hair on his forehead were the only things that distinguished his face from the white wall. Finally, he opened his eyes and said just above a whisper, "I was at the police station. A young police officer walked into the hallway and, just a few steps from me, pulled out his service pistol and shot himself in the head. There was panic. I couldn't move. Other policemen yelled, pushed us, and screamed for help. The dead body was in a pool of blood on the floor and part of his skull and brain were everywhere. I hardly had the strength to walk outside. I want to forget what I saw, but it haunts me! Even now if I close my eyes, that terrible sight pops up and horrifies me again."

"He must be the one who placed an explosive under the wrong side of the house and killed the young Serb couple last night," Sanela suggested.

"God answered quickly this time," Osman remarked. "My mother-in-law is crying all the time, asking God to punish him."

"Do you know what happened to my Aunt Zlata Kovacevich in Dubrave last summer?" asked our co-worker Muhamed, looking at all of us. All our eyes turned to him. "One day last summer, just around noon, my aunt had not finished her ablution when Serbs broke down the door and entered her house. Several of them grabbed my aunt and pushed her out. The worst among them was a woman who screamed, cursed like a trooper, and locked the door behind my aunt. My aunt knocked on the door and asked only for her clothes, at least her scarf, but they would not open it. My aunt sat under her apple tree in her yard and cried for hours. Finally, she raised her hands and asked God to give those people who took her house what they deserved. After a few days, the cruel Serb woman climbed that same apple tree to pick apples. Somehow she fell from the tree and broke her spine. She couldn't walk through my aunt's house anymore and was in terrible pain. She knew that Almighty God had punished her. Now she is telling everybody that this happened because the old women cursed her."

I reminded my colleagues that, according to our faith, individuals are responsible for their actions and that God listens to the prayers of the oppressed.

The Packages

Even during the war, I had a happy day. One early morning the telephone interrupted my dream. Aida told me wonderful news that a college in Kentucky had accepted her and awarded her a scholarship to pay for her tuition, room, and board. Every cell in my body and my soul was filled with happiness.

Another pleasant surprise waited in Merhamet..

"I met your husband in Zagreb," said Mr. Bishcevic cheerfully. "He came from Austria and brought a letter and three packages for you and some money Aida sent to him from the United States."

The information that Mr. Bishcevic met Husein softened my heart and gave me goose bumps. I returned to my work, but my mind was with Husein, just the two of us together, holding hands and letting our eyes talk.

At the end of the workday, after each co-worker had left the office, Mr. Bishcevic pulled a white envelope from his pocket. "It is unbelievable! Husein brought a thousand American dollars, five thousand Austrian shillings, and a hundred German marks, and asked me to give it to you. I told him that it is ridiculous. What do you need all that money for? If burglars knew it, they would kill you. I suggested he keep the money and send only a little bit, but he insisted on sending it all."

Mr. Bishcevic gave me the envelope. My hand was trembling a bit as I signed my name. As a volunteer at Merhamet, the money Husein sent was a fortune. Mr. Bishcevic opened the door of the storage room and showed me three huge boxes, the three "packages" he told me about that morning. Two were for me, and one was for Husein's sister, Shuhra Saskin.

What do I need to do with these huge boxes? How can I carry them home? Everyone will see them, and they will attract too much attention. I was confused.

Mr. Bishcevic recognized the problem and decided, "I will ask our truck driver to bring the packages to your home tonight. It is wartime, so we must be very careful."

I grabbed my coat, placed the money in my pocket, and

glanced at the letter. *Oh, how happy I would be to see you, Husein. You were in Zagreb yesterday. You were so close to home and so close to the three of us. I haven't seen you in so long and miss you terribly. When will we be together again?*

Samir couldn't trust his own eyes when he saw all the presents. He walked around the house in his brand new boots like a cowboy in a Western. He tried on all the shirts, sweaters, and warm jackets his father had sent and couldn't make up his mind which he liked best.

The presents couldn't brighten Nana's sad eyes. She looked at the fabrics, touched them with her fingers, and silently moved them to the sofa. Even the green wool sweater and comfortable, nice-looking shoes didn't change the gloomy expression in her eyes.

"Nana, do you like your presents?" I asked after a few minutes.

"Ah, my dear daughter, my happiness disappeared with my Husein. The presents cannot fill my empty heart." She wiped her tears. "I am thankful Aida and Husein didn't forget me. They sent good presents. I pray that Almighty Allah blesses them."

Thieves

The next day I rode my bicycle to Dubrave, happy to share the presents with my sister's and my brother's families. When I entered my sister's house, her tired, lemon-colored face puzzled me.

"We barely survived last night," she explained. "Burglars attacked Alija's family, and I ran outside, screaming for help. I screamed for our neighbors at the top of my lungs. As one of the thieves shouted, 'Shut up, bitch, or I'll kill you,' a new Serb neighbor answered by shooting into the air. The thieves fired back. Oh my God! It looked like a real war. When our neighbors intensified their shootings, the thieves ran back to their cars and disappeared down the street."

"You are a brave woman," I said and hugged her. "I couldn't imagine what would have happened if you hadn't scared them away. I am proud of you."

"I couldn't even think straight. All I thought about was helping Alija and staying alive."

My heart was beating as hard as Dervisha's, and I walked to Alija's home. Even twelve hours after the break-in, Alija's children were still terrified. Satka, Alija's wife, hugged her children, saying, "They did not touch my sons, but they frightened them."

"There were three of them," reported Kemo, Alija's son. "They were armed and had black masks covering their faces."

"They ordered me to give them money and gold," Alija said. "I told them that I needed money too. If I had had the money, I would have left for Europe and wouldn't even be here." Alija put his youngest son, Emir, on his lap. "When it was obvious that we had no money or gold, one of them picked up the coffee table, another grabbed the television, and the third took the video recorder. But the shooting surprised them, and they looked at each other, dropped what they were about to take, and ran out of the house empty-handed."

"I couldn't sleep the rest of the night," confided Dervisha. "I covered myself with three warm blankets but shivered for hours. I expected them to return to my house later."

"You surprised them," I said, patting Dervisha's hand. "They became afraid when they realized that others in the neighborhood had weapons. They found out you were not an easy target."

"I worried about your family the entire night," Alija said to me in a tired voice. "We have each other here, and in every house there is a man who could respond, but who do you have there? Who would hear your screams and who would respond?"

"Don't worry about me," I replied. "I ask God for His protection and rely on Him."

I then shared the presents and walked home.

I didn't sleep well that night. Before sunrise I heard knocks on our door. When I opened it, I found Mehmed standing there, his face white as chalk, trying to catch his breath.

"I was worried about you and your family," he told me, wiping the sweat from his face. I poured him a cup of coffee, but he was too exhausted to pick up the cup.

"Why are you worrying about us? Do you have bad news about Aida or Husein?" I folded my hands and shivered.

"No, it isn't about them. I worry about you and Samir. A friend of mine, Ramadan, came to visit us last night. He said that the gypsy girl from our neighborhood who knows you went to the pub where Serb soldiers gather to drink. She asked them to go with her to your house to get money. She knows that your husband and daughter are abroad, and she claimed that you have money." By the time Mehmed finished speaking he was almost whispering.

Fear and anger overwhelmed me. I stood up, paced through the room, and glanced at Samir and Nana. They were still sleeping, so Mehmed and I could continue our discussion without being overheard.

"I don't like that at all," I whispered, struggling to hold down my fear.

"I don't know how you could defend yourself and your family." Mehmed paused. "They want your money. Where do you keep it?"

"I dug a hole under the apple tree in our garden and hid it in a plastic bag," I replied. My mouth was so dry I could barely pronounce the words.

"Bring at least half of the money into the house. When the thieves come with their covered faces and weapons, give them some money. The money could protect you, your son, and mother-in-law."

"All right. I will do that. But what if they come back for more?" I asked as I began to feel anger replace my fear.

Mehmed shrugged his shoulders.

We were silent for a while, but anger helped ideas brew in my mind.

"She wants to kill me for a few dollars? I am not going to give her anything. Not a single penny. I don't want to reward her." I took a deep breath, looking at the bottle of water on the table. "I will fill glass bottles with water and store them among the flower pots on my balcony on the second floor. The entrance door cannot be opened easily. As soon as I hear them, I'll run upstairs and hit them with the bottles. This is my home, and I have a right to protect myself and my family. I am going to fight," I asserted, as courage and determination begin to replace fear and anger.

"I expected that answer. I knew that God gave you a strong soul, but I don't know if that is enough. You cannot fight weapons with bottles," responded Mehmed with deep worry in his voice.

"Don't worry. I'll place my trust in Allah," I said, refilling Mehmed's coffee cup.

"I didn't hear Ramadan's entire story last night, but he is coming to my house this afternoon, and then I will learn all the details. I will let you know what I learn," Mehmed said. He placed his empty coffee cup on the table and stood up to leave.

I grabbed the hoe, went to our garden, dug up the money, took the whole bag of it into the house, and then placed the dollar bills in a book. I hid the shillings and German marks under the blankets in my bedroom. I filled the bottles with water, placed them behind the flowerpots, and sat on the balcony, hugging my legs as I placed my pounding head on my knees. I found myself imagining the bottles and flowerpots flying down on masked faces. I saw fire from weapons, blood, and death in my mind. I stood up, leaned on the wall, covered my face with my hands, and sobbed until my eyes became heavy.

Late in the afternoon I met Ramadan. He told me, "Yes, yes, the gypsy girl searched for a companion to come rob you." Ramadan took a quick look through the window and turned back to me. "Thank God, a former student of yours was there, so you are safe." He smiled. "He told that skinny bitch, gypsy girl, 'If you rob my dear teacher, I'll come and kill you.'" Ramadan repeated the soldier's words. "It was your former student who informed me of this in the first place."

The student's words melted my heart. I thanked God that he was in the right place at the right time. This was not the only time that one of my students came to my aid during the war.

*Chapter 6—***Courage**

*Courage is what it takes to stand up and speak; courage is
also what it takes to sit down and listen.*

—Winston Churchill

Ethnic Cleansing

The warm spring weather turned my wheat fields green and filled
my soul with satisfaction and tranquility. That beautiful grass of
God's bounty promised enough bread for our little family. I
embraced my role as teacher-turned-farmer and headed for my wheat
field.

I mixed pesticides with water, placed the heavy canister on
my back, tightened the belts on my shoulders and waist, and aimed
the foggy liquid at the young wheat. The breeze worked its magic on
the growing plants, which undulated like waves on the Adriatic Sea.
It also brought the sounds of missiles to my ears, which sent a chill
down my spine. I walked to another part of the field, but the same
tragic sounds followed me. I tried to ignore those sounds of death
and destruction, and searched in my mind and heart for the happy
music of my childhood, but the gray war clouds of our present life
covered my entire emotional sky. I couldn't feel any enjoyment in
the field and competed with the wind to finish my work as soon as
possible.

By the time I had finished fertilizing the wheat, I was soaked
from head to with the sweat of labor and anxiety. I stopped at my
brother's house on my way home to change my clothes and warm
my cold hands.

"Why didn't you call us for help? You are not a tractor,
silly," my brother admonished me with a smile.

"I knew that a machine would do it faster and better, but how
could I ask our cousins to help me with their tractors when it is
difficult for Muslims to buy gasoline? I'm glad it is done now," I

118

replied, looking into my cup of steaming tea.

"I planned to come to tell you some unpleasant news." The trace of a smile disappeared from my brother's face. "Two days ago an armed Serb soldier came here because he knew that you're my sister. He said that all of the fields of Muslims who left the Serb Republic have been taken and given to soldiers. He showed me the paper that claims that Husein's field is now his."

"What are you talking about? How could our wheat field be his?" I bit my lower lip. I stood up and walked steadily across the room. "I was born in this place and grew up on these lands. I remember the days when horses plowed the field, and the smell of the fresh soil at plowing time is still in my heart. Every year the field looks like a beautiful carpet. One year the soil is planted with corn, the next year with wheat, after that with oats and potatoes. The beauty of that field has inspired a strength in me that will endure as long as I live!" The tears began to run down my cheeks. I wanted to go back to the field and scream loudly so that all my sprouting wheat could also feel the injustice.

"I know, but what can I do against an armed soldier?" inquired my brother as his eyes blinked.

"I never expected you to fight him. It is impossible," I responded in a lowered voice. "I will try to search for justice. We lost our jobs, and now our property is being taken away." I paused. "Our house is also in Husein's name. Should I expect a soldier to come tomorrow to kick me out of my home as well? That is what ethnic cleansing means—erasing us from our homes and land, from the place where we belong." My voice rose to a shrill sound as I simultaneously said the words and wiped my tears away. Anger at the injustice had begun to push the fear out of my heart.

"Now is not the time for justice. Please, take your son and Nana and go to Austria to join Husein. Go from this hell," he ordered me with an intensity that surprised me. "Only God knows what you mean to me. I want to know that you are safe."

"This is my country, and I belong here. I will go through all the difficulties that my people go through. If nobody opposes injustice, it will never be tamed," I responded and lowered my voice. "I promise I'll be careful, and I am always asking for God's protection. Don't worry."

I left thinking, *Did the soldier really have a legal document*

119

that would allow him to take my field? Anyone who gave him the paper knows I am still here and have a job in Merhamet. Why didn't they inform me? My name is not crossed off in the registered citizens' book. Maybe the soldier saw the growing wheat and fabricated a document so he could take the field. I'll go tomorrow, inshallah, to find out.

The next morning I went to the Community Building and asked for the office that awards free land. "You are not from here. I can tell," explained a man in the hallway. "It is not easy to find your way in a new place. I am a new citizen here too, but I can help you." He showed me where the office was. "Good luck." I walked upstairs and smiled at the thought of being taken for a stranger in my own town.

As I opened the office door, I recognized the person in charge as the wife of a former colleague. Her unpleasant appearance surprised me, but I concentrated on my own problem and approached her calmly.

"I heard that my wheat field has been given to a soldier. Nobody informed me. I came to correct the mistake."

"Let me be clear. It isn't a mistake." She stood up, leaned toward me, and placed her hand on her hip. "Your husband, Mr. Husein Softic, left the Serb Republic willingly. We made the decision that all abandoned property must be given to Serb soldiers, fighters for the Serbian Republic. They have done so much for their new country. They deserve it!" she exclaimed gratefully.

Why didn't you reward the soldier with your own property? I thought but did not challenge her patriotic feelings. I wanted to highlight her mistake. "Can you give me a copy of the document, please?" I paused. "Husein's property is not abandoned. The wheat is in our field. I applied chemicals to the plants yesterday. How can you say that the field is abandoned?"

"I'll give you the document, but you cannot appeal it. Our decision is based on verified documents, and it is final," she quipped, handing me the paper like a snake biting with its venomous fangs.

"There can only be one right decision. You have your reasons, and I have mine. Do you know somebody somewhere who can listen to both sides of our story?" I asked knowing from the bottom of my heart that truth was on my side.

She and her co-worker looked at each other, and their lips

formed into cynical smiles. The co-worker responded, "Our Ministry of Agriculture is in Bjeljina. Ask them there." Her sarcastic words were empty, meaningless, like smoke from their cigarettes.

I mumbled to myself and stayed calm. They did not seriously think that Aisa Softic, a Muslim, would take her complaint to the Serb Ministry of Agriculture in Bjeljina, It would be the same as a Jew going to the Gestapo Headquarters to complain about the mistreatment of Jews.

I sighed, took the paper, and left the office. The entire world felt as if it were upside down. I sat on a bench under a tree in front of the building and read: "Soldier Djoko Curkovic has the right to take the abandoned field that belonged to Husein Softic." I rolled my eyes and bit my lip.

I have to do something. I cannot cross my hands and wait. I must search for justice for the generations who had the land before me and for the youth that are coming. Could I win this? Should I hire a lawyer to represent me in court?

I looked around and noticed, hanging under the moss-covered roof of the front porch, a sign advertising "Attorney at Law Danko Vojanovic." *I knew Mr. Vojanovic; maybe he would help me. Lawyers are like doctors, ready to help anyone in need.* I stood up and walked the few hundred meters to his office.

Mr. Vojanovic welcomed me. He read my paper, raised his head, and said, "Nothing is wrong with the decision. It is not easy to build a new country. We have to reward the brave soldiers. Your husband chose to leave the Republic, didn't he?"

I wanted to scream, to tear all his books apart, and throw the pages into his blind eyes and his stone face. In my anger I felt that there was no more justice in those law books than there was in his hardened heart. He was satisfied to use his arrogance to make his decisions. I clenched my fist, but I couldn't keep my mouth closed any more. "My husband didn't have a choice. Your soldiers prevented him from going to work. Do you think he wanted to leave his home, his family, and become a refugee in a foreign country among strangers? Can you imagine how he felt leaving his elderly mother who could die any day and who needs his medical and emotional help now more than ever? He also had to leave his wife and his thirteen-year-old son behind. This separation was more painful for all of us than pulling the skin from our bodies." My voice cracked, and a flame of anger ignited me.

He continued to talk, but I couldn't listen to him any longer. He had said enough. I took the false document, left his office, and took refuge on the same bench outside the Community Building where I had sat earlier that day. The lawyer's words still echoed in my heart, and my mind responded. *How can you grant your soldiers my property? Can't you see what you and your soldiers are doing to me, my family, my people, and my country? We need to reward soldiers who are building a country founded on blood, injustice, rape, and torture? Is that your justice? Dear God, You are just. Please strengthen my body and my mind and guide me to find justice.*

Just then I remembered Radovan Dushanovic, the lawyer who taught in our school when I was principal, so I decided to find him.

When I came to the Federal Building, the place where Mr. Dushanovic worked, I was exhausted. I gave him the paper and sat. As he read the document, his face began to turn red, and he shook his head. "This is ridiculous. Husein's field isn't abandoned!" He stood and walked through the office. "Mrs. Softic, I am ashamed of this letter, and I'm going to fix this terrible mistake. The field and the wheat belong to your family."

After a few weeks a letter arrived stating that the field was being legally returned to me. The joy of relief was therapeutic on my tense nerves. I went straight to my wheat field and walked around, touching the green stalks, breathing the special smell of the young wheat, and enjoying the soft music of the plants dancing in the wind. For a while I ignored all the troubles of the war and felt secure and peaceful. I pressed the soft grain, and a white liquid rolled down the knife-shaped leaves. Of all the crops that God created, nothing in my opinion is better than wheat. The Master of the Universe fascinated me. We are able to eat bread and make delicious meals from the wheat that grows from the ground. Those green fields were a life-giving gift from God. What a divine mystery life is! How could some people be blind to this gift and purposely close their eyes and hearts?

The Serbs gave their soldiers all of the "abandoned" Muslim fields. Even an attorney explained to me, "We have to reward the brave soldiers." I almost lost my life fighting for justice and my wheat.

Harvesting

I scheduled the harvest for July 3, eager to have all my wheat in our attic. Early in the morning a young man knocked on our door and greeted me politely, revealing teeth white as pearls. He looked familiar, but I could not tell why.

"I know you from school, Mrs. Softic. You helped me tremendously a few years ago when I hit the gym teacher. Do you still remember that incident?"

Finally, I recognized his pleasant round face and brown eyes. The curly dark hair that covered his forehead and ears and almost touched his shoulders gave him a different look. Memories of the conflict occupied my mind. I remembered the loud knocking on my office door. "He hit me on purpose," maintained the gym teacher. "We have to kick him out of the school! How dare he treat me this way?"

The same day I met the student, who stared at me with sad-angry eyes. "He pushed me first. In response, I hit him. We both made mistakes."

"Why did the gym teacher push you?" I asked softly.

"The teacher came into our classroom this morning and asked all students to go outside. I did not feel good and wanted to stay in. He came up to me, grabbed me by the shirt, and pushed me. I lost control. I am sorry," he explained, his eyes full of tears. "We have a big issue at home. My father found a young girlfriend and left my mother, my two sisters, and me. My mother does not have a job... My father is an idiot!"

I tried to comfort him.

"Please, don't call my mother. She has enough to deal with. Call my father." His voice was chock-full of sincerity and his eyes jam-packed with fear. He wanted to apologize to the gym teacher, but the teacher did not want to see him.

The gym teacher tried to get the student expelled from school, and a teachers' meeting was called. I explained that both participants in the conflict had made mistakes. I suggested that the student be allowed to stay in school, and emphasized his family situation. After a long discussion, many of the teachers agreed with my opinion and voted to give the student a chance to finish his high school education. The gym teacher never forgave me for that decision.

"Tomorrow our new neighbor, Djoko, is going to harvest your wheat," the young man confided to me, breaking our silence. "Djoko came from Croatia two years ago to join the Serb Army. He has a document stating that the wheat is his, but we all know that it is your land." He moved his hair from his forehead. "I heard that you lost your job, and I want you to have your wheat to feed your family. But don't tell anybody about my visit today."

I thanked him, closed the door, leaned on the wall in fear, and sensed trouble. My heart was thumping, and my palms were sweaty. I asked myself, "Should I harvest today? Djoko could come to the field with weapons. It could be a bloody harvest. No, no. All the wheat and fields on the earth cannot compare to a human life. I am not going to harvest today."

I called my cousin, my sister, and my brother, but nobody answered. Finally, I grabbed my bicycle, headed to the field, and prayed for a swift and peaceful resolution.

As I approached the field, I met my brother on a tractor pulling a wagon loaded with dozens of huge bags full of wheat.

"I was expecting you all morning. We harvested almost two thirds of the field," he shouted over the tractor's engine, pairing his words with signs. His tractor moved slowly along the unpaved bumpy road.

I ran to the field as fast as I could, leaning on the bicycle from time to time. It was the middle of the morning, and the hot sun's rays danced in the field like a skilled musician's fingers on a piano. The red combine roared in a corner, and more than half of the field looked like a shaven head. A tractor was moving slowly and several men, working as hard as ants, carried the massive brown bags, heavier than their bodies.

"*Mashallah*, it is a very good harvest. You will not go hungry," expressed our neighbor, Djevad Langic. His wet t-shirt was glued to his chest. He jumped on the wagon behind the tractor and lit a cigarette.

"Aisa prays, and God blesses her with a good harvest," said our friend Mirsad Kovacevic as he wiped sweat from his suntanned face. I thanked him for helping me and offered several bags of the wheat for his family. "My family is far away in Sweden," Mirsad explained. "They are safe there, but Sweden is a gentle version of jail for them. They miss home already—our people, our sun, and our fields. I miss them too." He paused. "I cannot stand it when my son cries, calling me to move to Sweden to be with them."

"Are you going to join them?" I asked as I noticed tears filling his eyes.

"I cannot go to cold Sweden and leave this beauty, this paradise," he replied, and the goodness that was within him radiated through a gentle smile. My heart agreed with him, and I sighed gratefully.

As the tractor pulled a wagon full of bags and moved from the field, I noticed a full grain bag on the other side along the border with the cornfield. I quickly walked over to pick it up. Suddenly, a tall man appeared in front of me as swiftly as a ghost. He stunned me with his cold eyes. Fear filled my body, making me stiff, unable to move. *He must be Djoko.* His whole body was still except for the dancing fingers of his hand holding an ax. *What will he do with that ax? Is it too late to run? Is this the end for me?*

For a moment he was silent too. My knees shook as I glanced at him. On top of his short, straight brown hair were sunglasses. His wide, wrinkled forehead was covered with drops of sweat, and he wore a light blue t-shirt and brown shorts. As our eyes met, he opened his thin lips and white teeth appeared, inquiring, "Are you Aisa Softic?"

I nodded.

"You must be crazy! Why are you harvesting my wheat?" Anger was blazing from his eyes like heat from the July sun.

I collected my strength and answered softly, "This is my wheat. I cultivated it on my land, and I am harvesting it."

"I fought for this land. I left Croatia to build the Serb Republic, our land. The land is mine. What are my kids going to eat?" he asked as though I were responsible for his kids.

"I'll give you a few bags of wheat for your kids. I don't want them to be hungry," I replied, controlling my shaky voice.

"I don't want a few bags. I want it all," he roared like a lion.

"I lost my teaching job six months ago. I need this wheat to feed my family."

"Where is your husband? Is he fighting against the Serbs? Is he expecting that we'll take care of his family?" He screamed squeezing the ax, and I could see his muscles tense.

At that moment adrenalin took over my mind and body and my fight or flight response kicked in. I instinctively took a few steps back, my mind desperately searching for any place to run, my wild wide eyes focused on his ax, that sharp, cold tool. Bitterness filled my dry mouth and throat. I saw him as a wolf, and I was a sheep to be sacrificed. Fear paralyzed me, and I could not speak. My brain was blocked, and I couldn't even pray. I couldn't think about my children. The only thing I could focus on was the blood pounding in my ears. This was it. This was the end for me.

Suddenly, he moved a few steps back from me, the spasm in his muscles disappeared, and the wooden part of the ax touched the ground. His eyes blinked. "Our fight is not over. You will give me all the wheat. You may have it over my dead body. I am warning you! Stupid woman!" He was leaving the field leaning on his ax, looking like a three-legged beast. He became smaller and smaller until he finally became a black dot bouncing across the field with the other heat spots.

When I collected my strength, I walked towards my cousin Smail, who was still operating his combine thinking: *Oh Djoko, I cannot give you my field. My roots are deep here. I cannot be removed, like dirt, making your new country 'clean,' purely Serbs'. Your own sense of power and your weapons provoked you. You believed that it would be an easy task to eliminate an unarmed and innocent civilian population, but people stand up to your injustice.*

Smail turned the engine off and wiped the sweat from his forehead. "Did you see how Djoko jumped on my combine? He was ready to hit me with his ax. Every second I thought it was the last one. He almost killed me!" Smail paused. "Finally, I found my rifle, and I was ready to shoot him."

I thanked God that blood had not been shed on our field. "If you kill a Serb soldier, all the Muslims in the village would pay the price with their lives." I voiced, barely moving my glued lips and tongue.

My legs would no longer support me, so I climbed on one of the wagons and, surrounded by the bags, I bounced to their rhythm moving on the unpaved side roads toward my home. When one bag bumped my head, all of Djoko's words buzzed again in my ears, causing my frightened heart to skip a beat. I needed air, so collecting all my strength, I pulled myself up to the top of the pile of wheat bags. The completely or partially destroyed houses along our way grabbed my attention, and I counted them one after another. Without windows or roofs they looked like ghost homes. I had known their owners and remembered their family members, and their voices echoed in my memory. Once they crossed the bridge spanning the Sava River, they became homeless refugees that traveled through the world crushed and empty, like the abandoned houses they left behind. I was stuck between two hard choices: to join a river of refugees or to stay and fight constantly for my rights and for my life and the lives of my family.

It was nearly sunset when we arrived home. My brother and his friends carried the heavy bags up the steps into the attic. When the last bag was stored, I filled bowls with fresh-cooked cheese pita and gave it to them as supper for their trip home.

The wheat brought with it an unpleasantness of fear and discomfort. I sensed trouble, and I made Samir go with my brother to his house for a couple of days. I locked the doors and pulled the blinds down, but I couldn't find peace. I was crushed by distress and fatigue, and tears ran down my face. I knew that only God understood my fear and lowliness, and I prayed, *Dear God, please give me the wisdom to understand my role on earth. Is my task to fight for my wheat? What should I do if Djoko comes tonight to bomb my house? I am so frightened and powerless. I feel as if I am a single grain of wheat, unable to defend myself. Please protect me and let peace rule in all the fields and homes. Thank you.* The prayer took some fear and stiffness away from me, but I couldn't close my eyes.

The morning sun revealed dust and bits of chaff that had dropped across the floor when the wheat was taken to the attic the previous day. So I started to clean. My dear neighbors, Seka and Muharema, helped me. In the late afternoon, as we were placing clean curtains on the windows, a knock on the door interrupted us.

I glanced through the curtain and noticed three unexpected visitors. When I recognized Djoko, my heart almost stopped. He was in uniform and had a rifle slung from his shoulder. His face was dark red, sunglasses hid his eyes, and he was leaning against the house.

He was accompanied by an elderly man and a woman about

my age. She held a purse in one hand and moved her straight black hair from her forehead with the other. Her eyes held anger, and I had the impression that I had met her somewhere before.

As I opened the door, instead of greetings, the woman stated, "We've come to help you, Mrs. Softic." She looked at me keenly. "Soldier Djoko has a document saying that the wheat is his. I am suggesting that you willingly give the wheat to him. He counts on the wheat to feed his family." She obviously disliked me.

"I told Mr. Djoko that he could have a few bags for his children." I paused. "Mr. Djoko, I received another letter stating that the wheat is mine. I harvested it yesterday. The wheat is in my attic now." I looked at their angry eyes.

"I have the letter from last fall, and I haven't received any document about the wheat this year," informed Djoko, "but I know who sent the letter to you. When I finish with you, he will see who is joking with a fighter for the Serbs. I will reward him." His words were a bit slurred, and there was a strong smell of alcohol on his breath.

"You will regret your stubbornness," the woman shouted. "I have proof that we warned you. If you want to stay alive, you'll give the wheat to Djoko."

"Mrs. Softic, we know you as our good citizen," the old man told me, climbing one step up. "That is the reason why we came to talk to you. We have other methods to take the wheat from your attic. It is in your interest to give the wheat to him."

"I am really sorry that we cannot understand each other," I responded. "It is as if we speak different languages. I have told you that the wheat is mine, and that is the end of it."

"All right, we tried to solve the problem peacefully, but obviously it did not work," asserted Djoko as he moved away from the door. "If language doesn't help, I know what will. It is your choice, foolish woman, not ours."

"I thought you were intelligent, but you are stupid," remarked the woman as she turned to leave. "Yes, you are stupid. We gave you a chance. You made a bad choice, and now you will have to live with the consequences." I couldn't recognize their words any more as they walked down the street, growling like hungry brown bears. My skin chilled, and I locked the door.

I sat in my room for a while, feeling like chains were

tightening around my chest. I needed fresh air and went out onto the balcony that overlooked our garden. I leaned my tired body on the balcony's still-warm railing. The evening was quiet and the sky clear. As the bright stars appeared and beamed peaceful light, I thought, *This war is transforming our homes into fortresses. How can I find a bridge out of the fortress? We could all be destroyed by hatred.* I paused. *Only faith and love can guide us toward a path of understanding. Dear God, guide me to choose a good path to help me overcome my own weaknesses. You are one for all of us.*

When I needed fresh air, I went out onto the balcony that overlooked our garden. I leaned my tired body on the balcony's warm railing.

The Night in the Cornfield

Humans transgress all limits when they feel that there is no one above him.

In the beginning of July1993, the news of our neighbor Mirsad Kovacevic's death spread like wildfire, consuming all joy of life and suffocating the entire the village of Dubrave in grief. . I wanted to scream at the top of my lungs to shake and rattle all who were bent on injustice.

I walked through the house with my heart as hard as a sunbaked field in July. Suddenly, several knocks on my window redirected my thoughts and sorrow. My neighbor Mina was motioning me to come outside. When I approached her she whispered, "Today is our Judgment Day." She wiped the sweat from her forehead and looked around. "One of the Serb soldiers has been wounded in battle today. If he dies tonight, the Serbs are going to kill all of us."

"What should we do?"

"Run and hide in the cornfield. We cannot wait at home for our murderers to come."

A chill gripped me. Samir, my fourteen-year-old son, had not yet returned from my sister's home in Dubrave, and my mother-in-law could not walk as far as the cornfield.

"Wait a minute!" I raised my hand. "Wait! I must see to my son and Nana."

I ran to the garage, grabbed my bicycle, and pedaled as fast as I could toward Dubrave.

Dear God, protect my son and guide him safely home, I prayed. *Please protect him, protect him, and protect him*, I repeated with each push of the bicycle pedals. After about fifteen minutes of riding I noticed Samir and the invisible chains that had bound so tightly around me fell away.

"What happened, Mother?" He was staring wide-eyed at me. "Where are you going?"

"I came to find you," I explained with a sigh, placing Samir's heavy milk containers on my bicycle and quietly thanking God that my son was safe. When I told him the news about Mirsad, the muscles of his face stiffened and fear filled his innocent, youthful eyes. War robs children of their sense of security.

When we entered to our neighborhood, Samir frightened as a rabbit, looked around and whispered, "Mother, hurry up. Hurry up. It looks like all our neighbors have left their houses."

"You must go with Mina's family." I looked at his eyes. "I'll join you in a little bit."

"Mother, please go with us," he whispered.

"Come out with the child immediately!" I recognized the strong voice of old Mehmed, Mina's father.

I signaled for Samir to go and opened the window. "What can I do with Nana? I must…"

"You must leave Nana," pleaded Mehmed. "You cannot sacrifice your life and the life of your child."

I said my evening prayer, lit a candle, and sat on the sofa close to Nana. Her shoes were delicately tied in her scarf. I looked at Nana, looked at the shoes, and thought, *Can I ask Nana to put the shoes on and carry her on my back to the cornfield? Could I push her in a wheelbarrow? How could we cross the ditch? Nana could fall and break some of her bones. I need to leave Nana and the shoes where they are.* I pulled the door closed behind me. *Dear God, protect us. We are powerless.*

The coming night had begun to wrap itself around our small world and our great fears.

"Hurry up!" Mina whispered from her garden gate.

"I will stay here in my garden tonight," I confided, almost in tears. "I have to come back to check on Nana. I cannot leave her alone."

"I'm angry now," Mina moved closer to me. "Look, she has seven children. Two of her sons have been abroad for years. Why didn't they take her with them? It isn't fair."

"All of life is a test. Helping others brings blessings upon us," I replied. "Nana has lived with us for twenty years. She is the mother of my husband. She helped raise my children. I must protect her. But how can I do it?" I spoke hopelessly through my tears.

As though to make my decision for me, Mina grabbed my hand and yanked me forward. We hurried through our gardens as the last of the evening's golden light disappeared below the western horizon. Darkness and fear, its twin companion, walked with us as we moved quietly toward the deep ditch that separated us from the cornfield where we would lie in hiding through the night. I glanced back at the homes we had left, homes, which, in the ambient gloom of the night, had a look of sadness about them. Only one of them had a sign of life—one window where the flame of the candle I had lit sent forth its ray of hope. One small dancing light accompanied Nana as she sat in the house infirm and alone.

Oh, my dear Nana, forgive me tonight, I apologized from the bottom of my heart. *I couldn't take you with me, but my heart is aching at having to leave you. I couldn't even tell you that I left. How are you going to spend the night alone? You were afraid to sleep by yourself in your own room. Tonight you are alone not only in your room and in our house, but also in the entire neighborhood. Please forgive me. O merciful God, protect Nana tonight.*

"Aisa, hurry up," Mina whispered from the other side of the ditch.

I closed my fists, ran down the ditch, jumped over the narrow stream, grabbed some sturdy plants, and pulled myself up the bank. Mina grabbed my hand and helped me to the top. In front of us was a field with dark green corn stalks moving gently like waves on the Adriatic Sea. We reached Mina's family and Samir, sitting on blankets close to one another. I squatted next to my son and brushed his curly hair with my fingers.

"I hope we are safe here," whispered Nijaz, Mina's husband. "Our crazy Serb neighbors cannot cross the ditch in their cars to find us."

"This is ridiculous," Mina declared, raising her voice a little bit and turning toward her husband. "You can do what you want, but I'm going to get the documents I need and leave this hell with my children as soon as possible. I don't feel safe in this field. I want to be in a home or shelter far from bullets!"

Suddenly a warm wind brought with it a burning smell. A huge fire in the direction of our houses almost blinded me. I jumped. "Fire! My house is burning! Nana is there! Help! Help!" I screamed, running through the field.

"That isn't your house! My barn is burning! My poor cows!" Old Mehmed wrung his hands.

"You are both crazy tonight," Mina determined, standing in front of us. "The fire is far from our homes." She put one hand on her hip, and the other pointed in the direction of the fire. My eyes followed Mina's hand as it confirmed our error, but even so a cold sweat covered me and I began to shake. I grabbed Mina's cotton bed sheet and wrapped myself in it. Mehmed was whispering prayers.

A deep, frightening darkness and moist chill spread through the field. I heard rifle fire in the distance and the gunshots sounded as though they were getting closer. The cries of children echoed in the cornfield. I stood up and paced a few steps. All of a sudden the voices of several men and human footsteps from nearby paralyzed my breath and stiffened my muscles. It looked like they were only a few meters from us. Instinctively I cowered behind a row of corn. Mehmed placed the white sheets under an empty basket and touched a finger to his lips for silence. We stayed still, with only our eyes moving, darting around in the darkness. As the voices became louder, drums sounds in my ears played faster. I closed my burning eyes, frightened at the thought of what I would see when I opened them. Breathing slowly through parted lips, I felt like a speck of dirt in the huge cornfield, unwilling to accept all of our tragedies but too weak to take control of our destinies.

Are they going to slaughter us? I asked myself without moving my lips. *Oh, no the children! Dear God, protect our children, all children, and protect all of us tonight. Make us invisible to our enemies.*

Then as quickly as they had come, the voices and sounds vanished, and I could breathe again. The children, exhausted from the tension, finally nodded off to sleep. I thanked God. My heart softened, and I found a little bit of peace. Eventually I fell asleep.

Roosters spread their songs through the entire field. The dawn's calm light appeared from the darkness. Mina and I woke the children, and we all slowly walked home. I found Nana sitting on her sofa, moving gently from side to side. Samir lay down close to her, curling his knees to his elbows.

"Oh, I had a terrible night," Nana told me, still rocking. "The candle light vanished. I felt like I was by myself. Why didn't you answer my calls?"

"I couldn't hear you," I responded and looked at Nana's still fearful eyes as tears ran down my cheeks. I cried not only for myself and my family but for all those who loved our country of Bosnia more than their lives, for the millions of my fellow Bosnians who were spending fearful nights hiding in fields, for their burning and destroyed homes, for children who cried in shelters far from their motherland, for orphans without care. I cried for the death of mercy and compassion, consideration and love. In their place ruled hate and cruelty.

In July of 1993, Samir and I spent the night in this cornfield with Mina and her family. All of our Muslim neighbors spent many nights in cornfields.

Preventing a Catastrophe

I drank coffee and took a shower with barely warm water so I could go to work. In front of the Merhamet office Mr.Bishcevic walked toward me and informed me, "Aisa, you need to go to the Federal Building immediately. The minister, Ranko Borkovic, asked for you twice already." He paused. "It looks like something serious is going on."

I headed towards the ministry office. My legs protested the entire way and I wondered, *Why is Mr. Borkovic calling me? He is my former colleague from the high school. We teachers used to spend our breaks together and Mr. Borkovic would share jokes with us. But now there is a war going on, and it is not a time for jokes.*

As I entered the office, the minister's face looked like the sky before a terrible storm. He stood up, whispering, "We have to prevent a catastrophe. Sit down, please." He paused. "Listen to me carefully. Go to your attic, pack up half of your wheat in bags, and take it to the agriculture shop. Djoko is coming to pick up the wheat."

I looked at him in silence, regretting coming to see him. How could he tell me, after everything that had happened, to take my wheat to the agriculture shop? I was speechless until injustice touched my heart, and anger ruled my behavior. "The wheat is mine like these hands and these eyes. God knows that, and Djoko knows it too. I planted it, cared for it, and harvested it on my land. I will not give him my wheat. Period. I cannot do it." I paused for a few seconds. "I am tired of Djoko, of fearful sleepless nights, and of all of these pressures. He can kill me, but I will not surrender half of my crop to a threat." My eyes were wet with tears of frustration, and I stood up.

"Wait, wait, you are acting like a hero. Do you know how many heroes are underground now, dead from fights like these?" he raised his voice.

"I am not a hero. I want to live a simple life and cultivate my grandfather's land. Is that too much to ask?" He didn't answer, but his facial expression showed that he was listening. "I spent last night in a cornfield. Why?" I disclosed, almost crying.

"A stupid war is going on. Everything is crazy," he replied softly. "That is the reason I want to help you. Your life is more important than any wheat. If you need a bag of flour, I'll give it to you."

I sat again, covered my face with one hand, and wiped my tears with the other. I had lost the battle. "It would take me days to transport several tons of the wheat to the agriculture shop in a wheelbarrow," I stated, looking at the floor.

The minister made several calls. He put the receiver down and said softly, "Go straight home. People are coming to help you take it from the attic and transport it to the shop. It is important to finish the job today." He stood up and opened the door for me.

I left the office, and as I stepped outside, my eyes searched for a quiet, peaceful place to take a short break. A breeze brought fresh air from the Sava River, and I walked to the shore, talking to myself, *I could easily have managed my reaction, but this field is far deep in my heart.* I sat on a warm stone close to the water and looked at the shallow river waves, amazed at how they disappeared when they touched the bank. *Everything in this life is temporary, but rewards for our deeds are forever. I lost my battle, and I am going to give half of my wheat to Djoko. I don't want to, but I don't have a choice*, I whispered, watching my tears drop and make circles on the muddy water. As the small waves touched the gravel, I almost heard my mother's words: *Patience, patience, and patience.*

I came home and started cooking when five civilian men arrived. I recognized my fellow Muslims who had refused to join the Serb army, who had lost their jobs and had worked worse than slaves clearing the town of the destruction from explosions, as well as performing other needed tasks. Some of them also distributed food for Merhamet after work.

When I told them about my battle for the wheat, the tallest among them commented, "You did a good job to resist him this much. You did your part, and that is enough."

"It isn't time now to refuse a soldier's orders. He could kill you or your son," added one of them.

A truck came to our yard, and its engine sounded like a dentist's drill. The men sweated under the heavy bags, and by noon my attic was half empty. I served lunch outside for the tired, hungry workers. Then the truck left our yard carrying half of my wheat along with some of the pressure I had been under.

Exhausted from the night in the cornfield and the morning's unexpected activities, I couldn't rest. I filled a bucket with water, watered the thirsty flowers in my garden, and cleaned the steps in front of our house. A car stopped, and the minister of agriculture stepped out. *Now why has he shown up?* I was asking myself. *Does Djoko want more of my wheat? Does he want my garden? My other fields? Maybe even my house?*

"We prevented a catastrophe," he interrupted my thoughts. "Everything was ready, everything."

My heart pumped hard, and for a moment I wasn't sure what he was talking about.

"Go make me coffee. I saved your life." He opened and closed his fists several times, snapped his fingers and declared, "Like that! Just like that! Everything was ready to blow up your house." He smiled. "You would simply have vanished. The explosives were ready."

I thanked him for saving our lives.

Chapter 7—Sharing the Load

*Whatever life throws at us, our individual responses will be
all the stronger for working together and sharing the load.*
—Queen Elizabeth II

The Neighbors

I was lucky to live among the best neighbors in the world who
helped and protected each other. Late in the afternoon, after the night
in the cornfield, neighbor Ljubica called. "I heard you spent last
night in the cornfield. Come to my house tonight."

I couldn't believe that any Serb was ready to take such a risk
to help a Muslim. "You are inviting us to come to your house
tonight?"

"Yes," Ljubica's voice responded, firm.

"I have a problem. I cannot leave Nana at our house alone
anymore. Last night was—"

"—I am inviting Nana too," she interrupted me. "I want all
three of you to come."

"Oh, Ljubica! How generous. Thank you, and thank you
again." I was ready to accept the invitation, but I wasn't sure if Nana
would be able to walk to her house. "Let me talk to Nana and Sam ir,
and I'll call you back."

Ljubica truly amazed me, and her wish to help us brought
light to my tired eyes.

"Mom, Nana, let's go," Samir jumped and took Nana's
shoes from her sofa. "Tonight we can sleep in a bed instead of on the
hard ground. Let's go."

Nana did not move. After hearing our excitement about the
invitation, happiness failed to brighten her face, and she told us, "It
is a good plan for you and Samir, but I cannot go."

Samir came close to her, touched her hand, and maintained,
"Nana, your shoes are ready. Put them on and I'll push you in a
wheelbarrow. I'll make it comfortable. Please Nana, go with us,
please."

"Ah, my dear grandson, I don't want to make any trouble." Nana almost cried. "If soldiers see that Ljubica is protecting us, they'll kill her and her husband first. They'll kill us too. I am thankful for her invitation. May Allah reward her, but I don't want to make problems."

"We will hide you. I'll cover you with a bed sheet. Go with us, Nana, please," Samir begged.

"This is the third war of my life," explained Nana as she looked into Samir's innocent eyes. "I know how it works. You are young, and you don't know how cruel people can be."

"Ljubica wants to protect us from that cruelty. We'll be safe at her house," I asserted, wishing to change Nana's mind.

She turned her head toward me quickly and raised her voice, "You think like this child." She paused, "I cannot take my scarf off, just as you cannot take off your blouse. If a soldier sees me, he will immediately know that I am Muslim." She fixed her scarf. "You can go with this child. I'll be fine. If Allah allows them to kill me here, I am fine with that. I'll be a martyr."

Nothing Samir and I said could change Nana's mind. To stay in our home was her final answer.

I ran to Ljubica's house and explained Nana's fears and concerns. Ljubica admitted that soldiers had asked her why she chose green, a Muslim color, for the color of her balcony tiles and why she didn't hang the Serbian flag on her house. I was very pleased when she said that she feared only God and not the soldiers and that she really wanted to protect us in her home. On my way home, I thought about how the war exposed the true character of individuals. Some friendships did not survive the test of war. That test was like an x-ray that exposed diseased hearts, rotten souls, and fearful characters. Ljubica had not only exchanged neighborly greetings in public, but had opened her home to protect us. Her pure wish to help me and my family, despite the consequences, revealed the true nature of her friendship, and she obtained a huge, pleasant place in my heart. Even though I ended up declining her offer, her home was a safe haven that I could count on. For that, I would forever be thankful to Ljubica.

All of our neighbors were planning to spend the coming night together in the cornfield or in one house, but Samir, Nana, and I decided to stay in our home like three orphans.

Just before sunset, our neighbor, Ilinka, came to our home worried. "I have a big family, six of us, so it is not easy for us to find a place to spend the night," she confided quietly.

"I would love to have you here." My face brightened.

"We have enough space for everyone," Samir added, smiling.

"We could take turns guarding the house throughout night." Ilinka was confident. "My husband Djevad and I could be on duty from evening until after midnight. Your turn could be from then until dawn."

I agreed, and we implemented the plan the same night. At three in the morning, Ilinka woke me up, whispering, "Aisa, it is your turn to guard. It has been quiet so far. If soldiers come, call us."

The balcony door on the second floor was open slightly, and the fresh night air filled the room. I sat on a rug, leaned against the wall, rubbed my sleepy eyes with one hand, and covered my yawning mouth with the other. As I looked outside, I recognized the fence gate showered in the light of several bright stars. The sky was clear and peaceful. My ears caught the breathing echoes of the sleeping people and the sound of a wall clock above my head. Suddenly, footsteps coming towards the house chilled my body, and an abyss opened in front of me. Small quick footsteps approached closer and closer. I stood up, ready to sound the alarm. But I recognized the footsteps to be those of a dog trotting by our house, and my panic subsided.

I thanked God, relieved, and analyzed our defense plan, *How could we defend ourselves with empty hands? It would be impossible. If someone attacked us, we wouldn't have enough time to escape. I'd have to wake up eight people, help them escape into the garden, help Nana put her shoes on, and carry her before our attackers entered the house. The attackers would certainly have weapons.* I realized that only Allah could defend us. I started to pray, asking for Allah's guidance and protection.

The next night Ilinka came a little earlier with all of her family members except for Djevad. The sound of a distant shooting filled our hearts with fear, and all of us were quiet. When Djevad arrived after sunset, Samir locked the door and pulled down all of the blinds.

Suddenly the telephone rang. I barely understood Mehmed's whispers, as he shared that just a few minutes earlier he had seen a soldier walking on our driveway smoking a cigarette. With shaking hands, I put the receiver down and signaled for Ilinka and Djevad to come to the living room.

"Mehmed saw a soldier in our driveway." I whispered. "What should we do?" I moved my gaze from Djevad to Ilinka.

"That's not a good sign. Could he place explosives under the house?" Ilinka asked her husband.

"Let me see. I'll go outside and check," Djevad responded, walking toward the door. Ilinka stopped him. "Wait! Wait! He could kill you."

"I cannot wait for him to destroy the entire house and all of us," Djevad asserted, raising his voice.

"What can you do empty-handed? Wait!" Ilinka walked through the room. "A grenade killed our son. I cannot afford to lose you too!" Ilinka cried. We were absolutely quiet. "Call your sister. Ask her husband to come. He is a soldier."

"Wait a minute," said Djevad. He moved very quietly from window to window and peeked through the blinds.

"Can you see any lights? The soldier had a cigarette in his hand," I whispered.

Djevad stood up. "Wait a minute, I was smoking as I walked over here tonight. It was me, not a soldier. Mehmed wasn't able to make out who it was in the dark," suggested Djevad as he smiled from ear to ear. We all smiled and finally began breathing normally.

I called Mehmed and explained who the "soldier" was. For the next few nights we called Djevad a soldier.

One afternoon, looking very somber, our neighbor Safet Alijatic came along with his wife and daughter to our home. "We are leaving as soon as possible," he announced in his rough voice.

"Where you are going?" Samir asked.

"It will be a tough journey, and we will need a lot of strength and many blessings to stay alive," he told us, pausing and looking at his hands. "We are going to Travnik to join the Bosnian resistance fighters." Raising his head, he looked at us. "I cannot wait for someone to come and kill me, my family, or my neighbors. The police openly declared that they couldn't protect us. I am going to fight soldiers, not civilians. If Allah wills that I should die, I will be giving my life for my country." He paused again and in a lowered voice, confided, "We are sharing this only with you. As far as everyone else is concerned, we will be going to Denmark."

"You made a good decision," Nana praised him. "If nobody opposes injustice, it will run rampant. May Allah be pleased with you, and make your path easy."

At the end of December, just a few days before the beginning of 1994, my friend Aisha called. I hardly recognized her devastating voice. "We barely survived last night." She paused. "Somebody activated an explosive in front of our apartment. Thank God we are alive. We are waiting for the Red Cross to come to evacuate us." There was a deep sadness in her voice at the reality that somebody had driven her and her family from their home.

After a few months our neighbors Safeta and Nazif left their home and went to central Bosnia with their families as refugees. Our neighborhood was almost empty now.

Hurt Feelings

Early in the morning of August 2, 1993, a number of brutal crimes were committed in the village of Liskovac. Serbs shot Emina Turan in her yard. Her son, Almas Turan, was tortured and died in Banja Luka's hospital. His five-year-old daughter had to tell the story because her mother was not quite sane following her horrific experience. The same morning a similar brutalization happened to their neighbors, the Rizvanovic family.

Merhamet became a center where people, running from fear, searched for suggestions and comfort. We arranged a meeting in the local Red Cross office with the representatives from the village, the police, the local and International Red Cross, the imam Mr. Sheper, and Merhamet's representatives.

At the meeting the frightened villagers told their stories of terror and asked Mr. Larry Holigot, the representative from the International Red Cross, to help them leave the village as soon as possible. They wanted to go to Tuzla, Zenica, Croatia—anywhere to save their lives. Mr. Holigot informed us that nobody wanted to accept 3,000 refugees at that time. He asked the Serbs' representatives to ask Gradiska's police to protect Muslims. I couldn't believe my ears when Dusan Marovic, my former co-worker, said that the regular police could not protect the Muslims in our town and villages. That meant that Bosnian Muslims in Gradiska's county were unprotected, targets for hunting, worse off than wild animals. My heart was ready to explode, and I couldn't speak. The Serbs representatives insisted that the villagers from Liskovac pay all their bills and obtain the "proper" documentation before they could leave.

The next morning an Adventist Church leader and his wife, Djurdjica, paid me a visit. I was glad when they decided to fast voluntarily in the Muslim tradition, with no food or drink from dawn until sunset, and pray to God to protect Muslims. Fasting during month of Ramadan is one of five requirements of the Islamic faith, but some people decide to fast other days during year to come close to God. I invited them to come to my home at sunset so that we could break our fast together.

After we finished supper, I left my guests alone to perform the prayer. When I returned, I found them in different seats, moving their eyebrows and glancing each other. The minister broke the silence. "If you want to save your life, your house, and your property, you are welcome to accept Christianity as your religion. We will see about the procedure and also about how to change your name."

It was like thunder from a clear sky. "I cannot do that," I asserted with conviction and a bit of anger. "My religion is worth more to me than any of my property. I can only live as a Muslim and as Aisa. My religion is a part of my very existence—my guide to eternal life in the presence of Allah." I paused. "Would you have suggested to the early Christian martyrs that they give up their faith to save their lives?"

"I am sorry if I hurt your feelings. I only wanted to help you," the minister responded, looking at the floor.

"It does hurt my feelings. My religion teaches me to help my family, my neighbors, to control my actions, and to be a good person."

They apologized one more time and left.

My Wounded Brother

Toward the beginning of September my cousin, Fahrudin Cimirotic, got married, and I attended the wedding ceremony at his house. I met many of my cousins and friends there. Several Serb soldiers came to congratulate the newly married couple. They ate, sang, danced, and several times fired their rifles in the air. They projected an aura of superiority, an awareness that they had the upper hand, and a sense of power. I was afraid they had just come to cause trouble.

My hands sweated, and my throat became tight. I pedaled my bicycle hard on my way home, but anxiety traveled with me. Unfortunately I didn't find comfort in my own home.

Around ten o'clock that night, the ringing of the telephone scared me. Satka shared, just above a whisper, "Your brother has been wounded." She cleared her throat. "The bullet tore some muscles in his chest, but praise be to God, the wounds are not life threatening." She paused. "He is at the hospital—safe."

Tears showered my face. "Is he in surgery? I'm going to see him!"

"Please don't go now, at this hour of the night. You cannot help him. Trust me, he will be all right," she pleaded.

She took a breath and continued, "It happened at our neighbor Djevad's house. After the wedding I stayed to help clean up, and Alija and our sons went straight to Djevad's house to sleep. Suddenly, as we heard the rifle shooting and women and children screaming, we ran to Djevad's house. I found our sons, Kemo and Emir, and daughter, Amra, surrounding Alija, all four covered in blood. I did not know who was wounded or how." She cried. "What a traumatic experience for all of us, especially for our children! I am worried for their mental health. We have to leave this hell as soon as possible. I am afraid that it is already too late!"

"The health of your family is your number one priority." I reached a chair slowly.

As soon as Satka and I finished our conversation, I dialed the hospital surgery. The nurse, my former student, recognized me and connected me to my brother.

"I am okay, thank God," my brother told me. "A doctor said

146

that I am very lucky. The bullet missed my heart by only a few centimeters."

Tears of relief flooded my face as I listened to Alija. "We cannot thank God enough for protecting your good heart," I said. "I'll stop by in the morning to see you."

I went to the balcony. The sounds of distant missiles and rifles interrupted the moon's peaceful light. The warm night wind moved the leaves on the fruit tree in our garden and created a sound similar to my brother's voice. *Dear God, You have knowledge, power, and wisdom. Thank You for saving my brother's life. Please heal his wounds and keep him and my nephews healthy.*

When the roosters' early songs announced the coming dawn, I stepped back inside the house to prepare for the day. The sun's light was still making its way above the horizon when I left for the hospital to visit Alija. Chills covered my body when I saw his pale face and tired eyes. It was horrible thinking about just how close Alija had come to his death. I hugged him, and tears rolled down my face. I was glad that we were able to celebrate life and hug each other.

"The doctor took the bullet out of my arm." Alija pointed to the white bandages.

"What about your chest?" I moved the white cotton sheet from his healthy left arm.

"All that extra food I ate built a layer on my chest and protected my heart," Alija joked. "When I go back home from the hospital, I'll have a good reason to eat more."

"Thank God, you survived!" I proclaimed, looking at my brother's bright green eyes.

"I didn't expect rifle fire. But look at what a soldier did through the locked door." Alija paused, raised his head toward me, and whispered, "I didn't sleep all last night. I analyzed our situation and concluded that we cannot survive here. Soldiers can come and kill us whenever and wherever they want with no reprisal. I have to save my family and myself. We are going to ask the International Red Cross to help us leave, but I worry about you. Do you want to go with us?"

I blinked several times to keep from crying and told him that we will stay in our house.

Alija's wound had not healed completely when he returned

home from the hospital. His life was in danger because they thought the soldiers would come back. The International Red Cross scheduled a date to drive my brother and his family to a refugee camp in Croatia. On the morning of their departure, I took my bicycle and went to see them and to wish them safety on their journey. On my way I thought about my brother and our time growing up. I remembered my mother's last words to me, "When I finally close my eyes forever, take care of your brother."

Dear Mom, how can I take care of my brother now? You didn't know, when you charged me with that task, that war would come to us. I love him, and I want to keep the promise I made to you, but I'm having trouble protecting even myself. Alija had a very close brush with death, and I am thankful to God that he survived. I am going to miss him, but it is better for him to find a safe place for his family.

The entire neighborhood came to wish Alija farewell. The people wiped tears from their faces and sobbed as they looked at Alija, Satka, and their sons and daughter.

Kemo sat next to me. "Aunt Aisa, why are you crying?"

"I don't know when and where I'll see you again. I am going to miss your bright blue eyes and your smiling face, and I won't be able to be there for your birthday." I replied.

"I want to come back and celebrate my birthday with all of you," Emir told me. "Aunt Dervisha is going to make a delicious cake."

"I'll be glad when the war is over, and we can all come back home," Amra shared.

A jeep with a Red Cross sign came to the yard and interrupted our conversation. Everyone went outside wiping their tears. Aunt Mina cried loudly.

"Please don't cry Aunt Mina."Alija hugged her. "Unfortunately, I must leave my home and all of you. We will see each other again, *inshallah*."

"Ah my son, I am not sure about another meeting in this world. Forgive me for my shortcomings."

Alija's chin quivered, and he wiped at his tears. He hugged his aunt again. Everybody cried. There were no words when I hugged my brother. Our tears spoke for us.

The jeep started moving from the yard and soon disappeared

from view on that foggy fall day. I stood in front of that dear house which once had been so full of laughter and love. My childhood home, the home where my mother had lived, and my sister and brothers, and later my brother's family—that home was now as empty as my heart.

A cold wind moved the old oak branches as if waving to me to come closer. I walked over and leaned on the tree trunk, and because of all my memories, I felt a headache coming on. The yellow and brown leaves were still gently touching one another, and several acorns fell onto the grass under the tree. The acorns from this tree had been my toys as a child. I'd pretend they were dishes or furniture for my imaginary characters. I made books and money out of the leaves, and I was content, wealthy beyond counting. Everything that I needed as a child I received in abundance from this tree. I remembered when my cousin Hayra, stood under it, shouting that I had gotten my first job. I hugged the tree, my hands not even reaching half of its circumference.

A few weeks later, Serbs occupied Alija's house and cut down our dear oak tree. I felt as if part of my heart had been cut out too.

The New Neighbor

In fall of 1993, my dear Mina and her family received several serious threats. After midnight a bullet shattered their living room window. A few days later someone tried to open the window of their bedroom where her husband, son, and father slept.

"Nijaz, get the rifle! Shoot him! Shoot him!" she screamed even though they didn't own a rifle. All of them screamed louder than any weapons. Whoever it was jumped down from the window and ran away.

The news that Mina and her family were leaving overwhelmed me. A day before her departure, Mina introduced me to a good-looking widow about my age, who was going to stay in her house. Her name was Cvjeta. Her two daughters were college students, and her son was a policeman. She was a Serb refugee who came from Croatia. Before the war, she had worked in Germany. She gave Mina 3,000 German marks (about $2,000 at the time) for the furniture and appliances.

Two weeks after Mina's departure I received a letter from her. Mina's description of their departure took my breath away. At the first check point at the bridge a policeman ordered Mina and her husband off the bus. He beat them and abused them, asking for their money. The policeman tore off their clothing, searching for where the money could be hiding, until he found the 3,000 German marks.

I read the letter to Mina's parents. "Wait, wait. How did the police know how much money they had?" Mehmed narrowed his eyes to determine the connection. He stood up, and the sound of his footsteps and the gentle whoosh as he exhaled clouds of smoke filled the room. Suddenly he stopped, tapped my shoulder, and whispered, "It must have been Cvijeta's plan. She got her money back. Look at that clever fox! It must have been her, nobody else!" He lit another cigarette. "Stay away from Cvijeta. She is dangerous woman."

"We should not mention that we heard from Mina and pretend that we don't know anything," I suggested.

"Mina wrote this letter to warn us to be very careful about what information you share with her. That woman could cause trouble for all of us," Mehmed delivered, raising his voice to a warning tone.

I invited Cvjeta over for dinner as a neighborly gesture.

"Your family is in three different countries. It must be hard for all of you. Of course, it must be temporary," she remarked politely.

"You can see my old and sick mother–in–law. We cannot go anywhere now. But, one day, I hope I'll be in America with my family." I smiled.

"You are still young enough to accomplish a lot. You are smart and educated. America is a good country, the land of success." She patted my shoulder.

"I studied Russian in school, and…"

She interrupted me. "Don't worry. You will learn English very quickly. I learned German in a few months." She blinked several times. "But what will you do with your house, gardens, and all of your property here?"

"We can help and protect each other like good neighbors. If you help me to be safe here, I can sell my house to you," I offered, playing with her greed. If there were a possibility that I would sign over my property to her, she would make sure my house did not get blown up. She would also make sure that I stayed alive long enough to sign the property over.

She opened her eyes and parted her lips. Glee and greed spread across her face. "Oh my God! I can combine Mina's and your properties. My children could have separate houses close to each other!" She stood up and contemplated through the window. "I am not sure if I'll be able to afford this very nice house and the huge property around it. How much are you going to ask for it?"

"I have to talk to my husband. The house is in his name. I am sure he'll lower the price if you protect us," I assured her.

"You are safe here. I'll protect your family the same way I protect mine." She smiled.

"We could make a payment plan. I'll give you a good percentage of the money before you go."

I remembered Mina's letter, and I couldn't listen to her anymore. The room started to spin around me. Fortunately she didn't look at me. Her gaze was on Mina's and our gardens, and she was bursting from happiness.

"Oh yes, yes, and I'll deposit the rest of what I owe in

151

monthly payments in your bank account. You can buy a house in America for your family. It will work well for all of us. This is fantastic!" she affirmed in her low voice. "I am going to lock up the house and move to Banja Luka to live with my daughters for the winter. I am going to come back in the spring, and I'll protect you," she claimed happily.

When Cvijeta left for the winter, I regretted that we hadn't all left with Mina's family. Their house stood without life in a deep darkness with fear surrounding it. Instead of the pleasant voices of Mina's family members, the cold wind howled around our fences, playing with snowflakes and carrying the sharp resonance of weapons and the ear-shattering sound of bomb explosions. For many nights in my dreams I called for Mina to take my hand and pull me to the other side of a ditch, but a river spanned between us, unbridgeable.

When I woke up in the middle of the dark night, in our cold house and the empty neighborhood, I prayed, *O Allah, there is no power and no might except Yours. I complain to You of my weakness, my lowliness, and my fear. O Most Merciful, I seek refuge in Your light and ask You to inspire me to take actions and perform them in Your satisfaction.*

The Sick Child

Our town, on the border with Croatia, the exit point, stood as a barrier for Muslim refugees from the western part of Bosnia who didn't have transit visas through Croatia. In winter of 1993, when the cold north wind was our frequent guest and temperatures reached the freezing point, our imam asked me to host three young men and a young lady, Belkisa, with her baby. I made a bed for the mother and baby in the warm living room, and the young men slept upstairs in the cold rooms. Belkisa and I cooked together for our now eight-member family.

Two days after the family arrived, my son Samir became sick. He ran a fever, had a sore throat, and couldn't eat. I boiled an onion, put socks soaked in alcohol on his feet to decrease his fever, placed oiled paper on his stomach, and made hot tea. But Samir didn't feel better for two consecutive nights. On the third day, early in the morning, I dressed him and walked with him to see Dr. Anka Dobromilovic, a pediatrician. Our families had been friends for several years, and I didn't have any doubt that she would help us out. I was positive that she wouldn't charge me, but I placed a hundred dollars in my wallet in case she was absent and we had to see another physician.

Once at the office, I wrote Samir's name on a sheet of paper, turned it in, and found a seat where Dr. Dobromilovic could see us immediately when she entered her office. Samir leaned his fevered, aching head on my shoulder as we waited. Several sick kids came in with their mothers.

"What is wrong with your son?" the nurse, Dushanka, asked me politely.

"He has been sick for two days. I tried treating him with natural remedies, but nothing has helped," I replied.

"We are going to help you, Samir." The nurse smiled.

At that moment I recognized Dr. Dobromilovic coming toward the building. I leaned Samir's head on a wall and stood up to hug the doctor or shake her hand. She glanced in my direction and then immediately turned away from me. We both became confused, disoriented. She took a few steps back and walked away as fast as possible. Rubbing my eyes, I looked at the middle-aged women's back to be sure I was seeing the same person whom I used to know. Her walk assured me that she was Dr. Dobromilovic. I couldn't believe my own eyes. My throat became dry, and I had a difficult time with my eyes welling up with tears. As I struggled to contrl my bitterness, I walked to the window, grabbed my paper, and placed it in my purse. I sat next to my sick son, and anger filled my heart.

Are you angry at me, Dr. Dobromilovic? Why? What did I do wrong? Did I kick your husband and you out of your jobs? Did I destroy your family's life? Did I kill your friends? Did I wound your brother? Did I take your wheat from your attic? Did I take your car? What would you do if your son were sick and if you are in my shoes?

I didn't know what to do. Obviously Dr. Dobromilovic wouldn't see my son. *Could we go to the children's ward of the hospital and ask for help there? What if there is another Dr. Dobromilovic there? How can I take my son to another town, to another place to seek help? We cannot travel by bus with our Muslim names on our documents. If we take a taxi, what do we do at checkpoints?* But I knew I had to find help for Samir. I squeezed my purse in one hand and helped my son to stand up with the other.

Dushanka came close to me. "Mrs. Softic, a new doctor will take care of your son."

I nodded and wiped my tears. As we entered her office, the doctor revealed, "I heard about you and your family. I am going to examine your son and see what kind of help he needs."

I was touched to find mercy from a stranger.

The Police

As I entered my home with my sick son, the screeching sound of a police car slamming on the brakes right in front of our house startled me. My heart pumped hard. I watched five policemen jump out. The front door shook with a violent pounding. I turned the knob, pulled the door slightly open, and stared into the five hard faces.

"Do you have any refugees here?" one of them asked sharply.

"Oh, oh, yes, I am hosting one family," I answered in a quivering voice, afraid like a rabbit surrounded by wolves.

"We have to search your house," the policeman announced, as all of them entered. Their footsteps on the wooden floor in the hallway sounded like thunder.

"How many are here?" asked the first policeman coming into my kitchen.

"It is one family, three brothers and a young lady with a baby." I was shaking.

"Why did you let them stay in your house?" A blaze of anger accompanied his words.

Looking at the baby, I stated, "I saw a young couple with a baby on the street in the cold. I let them in to warm up in my home." I paused, "This isn't the first time that I hosted refugees. Serbian families stayed in my house twice. They came from Croatia. I helped them too."

"It is not the same. This is the Serbian Republic, so we have to help our people, but we cannot help Muslim refugees. Do you know that?" He raised his voice. "These people could be soldiers. Did they bring any weapons?" He looked around the room. "Where are they?"

"Belkisa with the baby is here." I moved my gaze to my sick son. "I took my son to the doctor, and we came back a few minutes before you arrived," I explained, trying to find the best answer. "Belkisa, do you know where your husband and his brothers are?"

"They went to obtain transit visas for us. We couldn't cross the bridge and go to Western Europe without the visas." I noticed her trembling hands holding her baby. All of the customary

155

brightness and gentleness was gone from her face.

"Do you have extra medicine in your house?" The policeman stared at the china cabinet.

I looked at my sick child, and my throat tightened. "My son was sick for two days. I do not have anything to give him, nothing to lower his fever. I took him to the doctor today even though I don't have insurance." I felt pitiful and couldn't talk any more.

"We are going to search your entire house. We will see what you are hiding here," the policeman declared firmly and gave an order to his squad where to search. I didn't know what they were searching for. What did they hope to find?

Why did the policeman ask me about the medicine? What is their plan? Will they accuse me of being an illegal drug dealer? I had hidden all my money in the books upstairs in my room. For sure they will take the books. Oh, and I also have some religious books. Policemen and soldiers didn't like the books in which God's names are mentioned, especially if they are written in Arabic. Will they burn my books and perhaps my house along with them?

I don't have any weapons, but they could bring a few guns and "find" them in the house. The five of them are going to serve as witnesses against me. Are they going to take me to jail or kill me here? Will these be the last minutes of my life?

The room was spinning around me. I became cold as ice, trembling and shivering as if I were falling apart. Samir, Nana, and Belkisa looked at me. I stood up, walked to the window, and looked at the quiet garden. Belkisa joined me. Even the baby didn't make any sounds.

Objects, mostly books, were falling on the floor. The policemen's belittling laughter struck me. They sneered at all that they touched.

"Are those materials from your Muslim political organization?" asked one of them from another room.

I wasn't sure that I was able to shout back, so I walked to the hallway. I found him looking through piles of materials from Social-Democratic party meetings.

"I am not a member of any Muslim political organization," I responded, just above a whisper, my mouth dry and bitter. My tongue could barely move, and I wasn't sure he heard me well. *In the last election I choose to be on the Social-Democratic Party voting list. I wanted to prevent a war.* Collecting my last strength, I explained, "I am a congressional representative in our local government. Do you want to see the written materials?"

He turned his hands from the materials as if they were on fire, walked a few steps toward me, and opened his eyes wide. "Are you an active member of the government?"

I nodded.

"Do you go to the government meetings?" Frowning, his eyebrows touched each other. He came closer, trying to distinguish my weak voice from the noise that other policemen were making as they searched the house.

"Yes, I do. We have discussions on the last meeting…"

He interrupted me, "No, no, you are fine. You are fine. I am sorry—we made a mistake. This is our mistake," he told me softly. Suddenly he looked as if he was afraid of me, an unarmed Muslim woman.

"Hey, guys stop your work immediately!" he roared. "All of you! Put everything on the floor back where it was and clean up your mess. Did you hear me?"

Silence filled the house. The policemen picked up the books and straightened them.

"I am sorry, Mrs. Softic. I did not know that you were a representative of the government. You didn't warn us when we entered your house. How would I know that?" he paused. "We didn't harm you. We really didn't do anything wrong. Your rooms will be in the same shape as before our visit. You have unknown refugees in your house, and we wanted to protect you—to be sure you were safe. That is all." Suddenly his voice was as soft and gentle as though he were my guardian angel.

I was confused by the sudden change in the behavior of the policemen.

"Mrs. Softic, can you come to my office tomorrow morning, please, and register them? Bring the ID cards of the people who are in your house. They don't need to come with you. They can pursue their transit visas through Croatia, no problem. Poor people. Look what the Croats are doing to them! They are taking money for nothing. Everybody can go through Croatia without visas except the poor Bosnian refugees," he expressed, smiling.

The other policemen walked quietly through the house.

Nobody mentioned any religious books or money that they had found. As they closed the front door and walked toward their car, I ran upstairs. Everything looked as it had before their visit. All the books and the money sat in their right places. I thanked God for His intervention to help achieve this positive outcome.

After a few minutes the refugees came back into the room quietly.

"How did you disappear? Where did you go?" I asked.

"We jumped over the balcony fence and went into the garden. We didn't even want to cross paths with the policemen," divulged the youngest.

"Soldiers took our father, and he never came back," added Muharem, Belkisa's husband. "That day we jumped out the window of our home, ran to the woods, and thank God we survived."

"Did the policemen harm you?" asked one of them.

Belkisa stood up holding her baby and reported, "I saw with my own eyes how the policemen behaved as they came in and how they left the house. Aisa is a devout believer, and God protected us."

I went to the police station the next morning. The police officer was polite. He wrote down the refugees' names and thanked me for fulfilling my citizen's duties and registering them.

The Clear Sign

In the middle of May spring arrived with all of its beauties. My new neighbor, Cvijeta, returned to Mina's house and worked tirelessly in her garden.

As it was a warm Thursday night, I opened the window slightly. A breeze brought the smell of tulips and daffodils into the room and played gently with the curtains as a mother would rock a sleepy baby in her arms. I was making myself ready for the nightly prayer when suddenly Cvijeta's voice penetrated the open window.

"Aisa, could you come outside? Hurry, please, hurry up." She motioned with her hand and looked upset.

As I ran from the house, Cvijeta said, "A few minutes ago, two men exited my front door. They appeared to have left something under my car. Can you see it?" She aimed a flashlight at a piece of cloth that was under the bumper.

"Did you call the police?" I asked, looking at the confusion, fear, and anger in her face.

"Yes. They only drove past the house in their car. They didn't care and didn't even stop to see why I called them. Never in my life have I been angrier!" For a moment we were as silent as Mina's tree above us.

"What is it? What should I do?" She looked back and forth under her car.

"You could come to my house," I whispered, looking at her trembling hands.

"Oh, let me get a few items, and I'll come right over," she answered, running to her house.

I informed Nana and Samir about our guest. Then, rolling up my sleeves and fast as the wind, I cleaned the table, straightened the rugs, fixed the curtains, and dusted the china cabinet.

Cvijeta came over shortly, holding her heavy bag in one hand and covering her chin and mouth with the other. The curtain waved and touched her face, and she pushed it aside and peeked through the window. "I saw them, two of them," she explained. "They walked down the street toward your house." She came closer to me, and clouds of anger appeared in her brown eyes. She blinked, hid it inside, and continued to walk and to talk to herself. "Why didn't I shoot them with my automatic rifle? I wouldn't care if I had killed them. I had a valid reason—self-defense. They left their evidence under my car. They came onto my property. I should shoot them, shoot them. They deserve a bullet."

Her monologue scared me. I looked at her and her bag with suspicion. She came back to me, inquiring, "Why did they come? What did they want?"

"Gasoline. Do you have gasoline in your tank?" I was guessing.

"Gasoline? Did you say gasoline? I'll give them "gasoline" tonight. I am going to wait for them to come back. You will see," she announced, opening her bag to remove a handkerchief to dry her forehead.

Look at the chameleon personality! You want to kill the men for gasoline? Do you know how Mina felt when your friends took all of her money? You can't plant bad seeds and expect a good harvest. Why did you include me in your game? Are you going to shoot those men from my house? Dear God, stop her. Her plan is not good for us.

It was midnight, but Cvijeta was still pacing through the room, the eyebrows on her forehead moving. From time to time she looked through the window at her car. Suddenly she considered Samir, "If you give me your dog, I'll sleep in my house."

I looked at her puzzled. *Why did she change her mind? Is she afraid of us or of the Serbs that could attack a Muslim house? Why does she need our dog?* I didn't like her idea, but her shooting from our house sounded worse.

"Mom, what do you think?" Samir opened his still-sleepy eyes to inquire.

"Oh, I guess, that would be all right. We could give you our dog as protection for tonight." I sounded unsure and scared, but it was better for all of us.

"Oh, thanks!" she voiced, jumping up. "Your dog doesn't like me. Samir can bring the dog and leave her in my yard." She took her bag and walked to her house. Samir and our large German shepherd followed her.

When Samir returned, I locked the door and peeked through the curtain. The dog was standing close to the fence, looking at our house, like she was protecting us.

Cvijeta's unhappiness and fear rubbed off on us. I glanced at the yard several times, terrified that the men would come back. My heart drummed in my ears, and my hands shivered. If those two men were not afraid of Cvijeta's weapons and her policeman son, they could come and do as they wanted to me. They knew I was a Muslim woman, alone, with no weapons and now not even a dog. Fear gripped my heart, and I felt alone in the entire world. Samir and Nana slept, and there was a long scary silence around us.

I have to pray, and my prayers will be my weapon. I started to beg Allah for help and protection, and as I was asking Him for the last time, tears showered down my face.

Dear God, I am submitting myself to Your will, ready to follow Your guidance, Your direction. Please show me an understandable sign, let me know what I should do. If You want me to leave my home, I'll do it as soon as possible. If You want me to stay here, please protect me. Please protect my son and my mother-in-law. I am a weak, poor, unarmed woman with no control over my life or the lives of those two people. We don't have anybody to protect us except You. You are our only hope.

Those words accompanied by my tears were the most desperate prayer of my life. As I finished it, some of my load was lifted. I walked slowly to my bed and closed my eyes. In my dream I was in my house alone. Suddenly a soft, bright light grabbed my attention. It seemed to be coming from the second floor, and I walked upstairs to see it. Immersed in the light I felt warm, peaceful, and satisfied. I walked toward a big white door in the hallway and went outside onto the balcony. I was surprised to see a tall "porcupine fence" made of tempered steel on the street in the front of my home. I looked again to be sure that the fence was real. I rubbed my eyes, but the fence remained there. On the other side of the fence was a short soldier. I was so thankful for the fence that I screamed, "Hey, my house has a fence! You cannot reach me!" I woke up, still excited. I was in the same house but touched by the light, everything was different. Fear, my constant companion for the last few years, had disappeared.

Dear God, Your answer was quick and crystal clear. I don't have enough words to thank You. Keep me close to Your mercy and make me fear only You. Amen!

My home became my safe island, the place where I found peace and satisfaction. I had a noble and great purpose in my life—to worship Allah alone.

Husein's Journey

Husein had studied hard for his medical exam in Austria. When he told me on the phone that he passed the exam, rays of hope for a better life touched my heart, and I responded cheerfully, "Congratulations! You should investigate opportunities for a job there."

"I am going to try, but I have an accent and many other problems," he paused. "It will be hard for me to find a position here," he answered sadly.

"You passed the exam. You have twenty years of experience as a physician. You'll be fine," I encouraged him.

"I am afraid not only because I still have not mastered German, but also for your lives there and Aida's loneliness in the United States. Some nights I cannot close my eyes at all."

"Why do you worry about Aida? How is she doing?" I was surprised to hear she was having problems.

"Aida works a tough job in a nursing home, and still she saves money for us. Look how much money she sent. She is studying chemistry full time at Wright State University. She also worries about you and Samir a lot. I do not know how she is surviving. She is under a lot of stress, and her face does not look good. A few days ago she locked her car keys in her car. She called a policeman to help her. She does not have time to cook. I worry about her health." Husein's voice shook.

I was speechless. Aida always shared her happiness with me.

"Do you want to go to America and help her?" I sighed.

"I thought about it, but I haven't studied English. What could I do there?"

"You and Aida can help each other. She could help you learn the new language, and you could cook and be there for her," I suggested.

"Aida is busy with her school and her work. She does not have time to teach me English. In a few months I'll turn fifty, and I am too old for a new beginning. I don't know what to do. This war is going to destroy our country and all of us."

After a silent moment I shared my suggestion. "You can do two things at the same time. You studied German and passed the medical exam. If you want to benefit from that, search for a job in Austria. In the meantime ask Aida to send you documents for an American visa. If you find a job, you could financially support her and make her life easier. If you cannot a find job, when the visa is ready, go to America. Samir, Nana, and I could join you guys and finally all our family will be together."

Husein followed my suggestion. A few days after his fiftieth birthday he found himself a refugee in America. Half of my worries were gone, but still the fight for my house persisted.

Chapter 8—The Fight for the House

It takes hands to build a house, but only hearts can build a home.

—Author
Unknown

Our House Is a Target

Some people tried to take advantage of the war and plundered as much as possible. At the end of June 1994, I was coming home from work and noticed Cvijeta, standing close to the fence. Mina's pink, red, and yellow roses decorated the fence, giving it a heavenly appearance. I sighed, thinking of how much Mina had tended and loved her flowers.

Cvijeta, motioning for me, whispered, "Two men were looking for you this morning. One of them wants to take your house for his family." She became quiet for a moment. "They surprised me with all the information they had about your family. I defended you as much as I was able to, but it didn't work very well. For everything I said he had an answer. The younger of the two was very angry, even rude." She blinked several times and looked at my house.

I thanked Cvijeta and entered my home with an uneasy feeling. Samir gave me more details about the visitors' appearances. "One of them was in uniform and looked like Djoko. He was young, tall, and strong. He had a rifle and two grenades. The second man was much older and looked like he could be his father. He was short and didn't carry any weapons."

I told Samir that God was protecting us, so the men couldn't hurt us.

As I went to the garden to pick vegetables for lunch, a deep male voice startled me, calling, "Hello, Mrs. Softic!"

The two men came to inform me that they were coming into my house with their families. They were standing under the apple tree's shade while I was picking vegetables from the garden.

I raised my head and recognized the two men from Samir's descriptions. They were standing under the shade of the apple tree, a few yards from me. The young man, looking irritated, moved his straight black hair from his forehead to reveal angry, large brown eyes. In his military boots and fully armed, he looked as if he was coming from a battle. The other man adjusted his silver hair and tucked in his clean summer shirt.

"When are you leaving, Mrs. Softic? Tonight I am moving into your house with my family," asserted the soldier so vehemently that some of the apple tree leaves moved from the strength of his voice.

"I am here in my house, and I am not leaving," I disclosed, searching carefully for every word. "If you don't have a place for your family, you can come to my house. We have enough rooms for my family and yours." I came closer, and the horrible odor of alcohol and sweat filled the air.

The soldier frowned, cleared his throat, and asked, "Where is your husband? Why didn't he go to fight for his home and his family?" He fixed the rifle on his shoulder. "You have to leave this house. I need it for my family."

"My mother-in-law is sick and unable to walk. I cannot carry her," I explained softly.

"Why did your husband leave his mother here? Does he expect that we will take care of his mother? It is ridiculous!" He paused, looked at the house, and continued, "I don't care. I am coming tonight. The house must be empty! Did you hear me? The house must be empty!" The entire garden echoed, "Empty, empty, empty!"

The soldier led the way from the garden with the old man trailing after him like his shadow. I carried my basket tightly to my chest to muffle the sound of my beating heart. As we walked along the side of the house, the thought that Nana, Samir, and I could live in the unfinished basement occupied my mind. But after a few steps, my brain rejected it. *This is my land, my house, my life—I am not moving anywhere.* I became strong as the foundation of our house. *But I have to do something now, something quickly, to change the soldier's mind. Tonight it will be too late. Fighting is not an option for me. I have to do it with kindness. Dear God, help me!*

"Come into the house to meet my mother-in-law," I suggested kindly, opening the door. They followed me. Nana was lying on the sofa keeping her right hand on her shoes. She looked like a dead person with her closed eyes and wrinkled yellow skin. Her mumbling of Arabic words and deep sighs from time to time served as her only vital signs.

"Have a seat. I am going to make coffee for you," I stated, moving the chairs toward them.

"No, thank you," the soldier responded, walking backwards from my living room, keeping his eyes on Nana's face. It looked like Nana had hypnotized him. As he bumped into the hallway wall, he revealed, "Okay, I am going to search for another house. If I can't find one, I am coming back here tonight." His voice mellowed, and he kept staring at Nana.

"It is fine. I'll be here with my family." My words expressed my final decision.

As they left, I sighed. *I cannot leave my home. I cannot do it now. I offered him half of my house, but he refused. He wants the whole house. What arrogance!*

As the sun's light vanished, I became twitchy. My ears, like antennas, reacted to every sound in or around the house. Nana and Samir slept, but I couldn't relax and I couldn't breathe well from the pressure in my chest. I went to the balcony, placed a few pillows behind my back, covered myself with a light blanket, and let the memories swirl around me about how hard we had worked building our house and how much love we had put into it.

*   *   *

167

In the spring of 1977, Husein and I went to Split, a city in Croatia, and bought back to Gradiska a trunkful of cement. We invited many people from Orahova and Dubrave to help us build the foundation. My sister and I cooked tirelessly from sun up to sun down the day before the foundation had been laid. When Dervisha had gone home, I prayed for a blessed house filled with prosperous lives.

On April 23, on the ground on which our house would rise, 50 people worked like bees. Our old friend, Ramo, killed a lamb in God's name in the appointed corner of the house foundation and later roasted it for lunch. Mina, rolling up her sleeves, helped us to heat and serve food, and wash dishes. Not long before sunset, the sun's rays gently touched our foundation. From the bottom of our hearts Husein and I thanked all the people who helped us.

My mother and my brother, Alija, surprised us with their decision. "We will make bricks from your father's and grandfather's land. We wish the bricks will keep you happy and satisfied in your house for rest of your life," said Mother with a brightness sparkling from her blue eyes.

While we were placing tiles on the roof, we sang our favorite songs together in great harmony. The neighbors, hearing our singing, brought coffee and cookies as refreshments.

Husein put the final roof tile in place and announced, "This house is strong enough to protect us and keep us warm, not only for us and our children but also for our grandchildren. Why does every generation need to build a house?" He smiled. "We don't know what challenges our children will face, but having a place to live will certainly ease their lives regardless of what the future has in store for them."

We built our house and put so much love and effort in it. It was a nice, pleasant house. During the war it became a target for soldiers and refugees.

*   *   *

The ringing of the telephone returned me to the dreadful present. The clock on the wall showed a few minutes past midnight. I was afraid to answer it. When the telephone rang the second time, I waited a few seconds, then grabbed the receiver.

"Is there a Mrs. Kukavica?" asked the unfamiliar voice of a woman.

"You have the wrong number," I replied ready to finish the conversation.

"Wait, wait. Is this the house where the Softic family lived?" the woman asked.

"My name is Aisa Softic, and I still live here," I delivered, making it clear.

"Oh, Mrs. Softic, your house belongs to the Kukavica family. They must be there already, but it is not important now. I am calling from Germany to inform my sister that Muslims killed our brother today in fighting on Mount Igman. I am sorry for the late call, but I just heard the tragic news a few minutes ago."

"I don't know how I can help you." I was confused.

"She'll be at the house at any moment. Please inform her of the tragedy, will you?"

"If she comes, I'll inform her." I finished the conversation and walked only a few steps when the phone rang again.

I don't know how I am going to survive tonight. Who is the Kukavica family? Are they coming tonight? Did Muslim soldiers really kill their brother? Is this all a bunch of games and lies? I looked out at the dark, scary night. *Is the soldier who visited me today coming tonight with his family as well?*

I was angry, scared, and tired, but I picked up the receiver. "I am calling from Serbia. Our brother died today. Muslims killed him. Oh, is my poor sister there?" cried a different voice.

"I am sorry for your loss, but your sister is not here and I have never met her. I don't know how to help you," I responded, my blood beginning to boil. The calls smelled of foul play. I disconnected the telephone, sat on my bed, and put my painful head on my knees.

The sleepless night left me with a terrible headache. I walked to work rather than ride my bicycle, hoping that the fresh air would ease my pain. Just as I reached the office, a middle-aged man and a young woman approached me. They looked like father and daughter, based on their ages. The woman, moving closer, stated kindly, "My name is Nada. I knew you when you were the principal of the high school." She paused. "This gentleman is my cousin Milan. He came from Visoko, and he wants to talk to you about trading houses."

"Trading houses? I don't want to trade my house," I replied.

"You are right," Milan affirmed. "Nobody wants to leave his or her home. I didn't want to come here, but I didn't have a choice. May we come to your house to talk a little bit? I have many pictures, and I want to show them to you."

"You can come, but I cannot make any promises," I conveyed, walking toward the office.

"We don't want to pressure you. Trading houses is a big decision, but let's talk about that possibility." He paused. "When would be a good time to come?" the man asked, smiling.

Milan and Nada came at 4:00 o'clock on the same day.

"You have a nice, pleasant house. How do you keep the cool air inside?" Nada asked.

"The house has insulation," I explained. "I open a window early in the morning and let the cool air in." I poured fresh coffee into the cups.

"You will never be hot in my house," declared Milan. "Trees shade the house throughout the day." He opened a big envelope, took his glasses out, and pulled out the pictures.

The one-story house looked fine, and I looked at the pictures to be polite.

"Your house has two floors, but look at the buildings around my house. I have a summer kitchen, a smokehouse, a place for wood, a separate garage, and a well. Look at the well. Of course, we have water in the house, but in the summer we drink fresh cold water from the well. On our entire street only we have a well. It is a real asset to have one in your yard. It's worth more than some houses. All our neighbors come to drink our water." He paused, and happiness sparkled from his eyes. "All of that richness can now be yours." He placed the pictures on the table in front of us, sipping his cup of coffee. He didn't wait for my answer as he continued, "My wife is there, waiting for you to come. She is doing there exactly what you are doing here. We are smart. We don't want to lose our houses. Look at this war. Look at this stupidity. People are moving like flies, leaving their properties, and saving their lives. What would it be like to be homeless?" He became quiet, waiting for my answer as a measure of the quality of his speech.

"You spent time and a great deal of effort to keep all those buildings in good shape. It looks nice," I offered, picking up my cup of steaming coffee. "But I don't know anybody in your town, I've never been there." I paused. "I don't want to leave my home."

Milan frowned, his eyes looking somewhere far away, and stood up. He came close to me, and leaning on the table, he whispered, "We need to be very careful. Those soldiers want houses too. Some of them have never had their own houses. They see war as an opportunity to become rich. It is true what our Nobel Prize winner, the writer Ivo Andrich, said, 'There comes a time when smart people become quiet, the unwise open their mouths, and the homeless become rich.'" He stopped, took a handkerchief from his pocket, and dried his face.

He looked at me, and because he couldn't see excitement on my face, he continued louder, "Nobody asked us about the war, but we are paying the consequences with our lives and our properties. We don't want to trade our house, but the politicians decided to divide Bosnia into three parts. People must live with their own people or be killed." He stood up and walked across the room, lowering his voice. "I am not telling you all this to make you frightened or bitter, or to make you hate other people. I want to help you and me to save our properties through this terrible war."

I couldn't move and couldn't talk. *He really wants my house, I thought. He is making me nervous, and there is something unsettling about him. This is ethnic cleansing. He would move in here to live in a "clean" Serb Republic with no Muslims here. By trading houses with him, I would be helping him to accomplish his goal. How would I make it to Sarajevo's suburbs alive? The whole of Bosnia is under Serbian occupation except for the big cities, and there are established front lines. How would I cross the no man's land to get into Visoko? I am sure that nobody asked him to leave his home. He came here on his own free will to join in this ethnic cleansing.*

Reading my thoughts, he came back to sit and explained to me in a soft voice, "I liked my town and had a good life there. It is only forty minutes from Sarajevo. Your children could travel to college from home. You and your husband would find jobs immediately. With my good house, among your own people, I guarantee you would have a good life."

"My people are here. I've never been to Visoko, and I don't know anybody there," I replied.

"Don't worry. You'll thank me. We can find an attorney and make our changes official. You can go there, and my wife can come here." Milan's gaze moved through my house as he spoke, fixing his eyes on the garden, a happy smile covering his face. We exchanged telephone numbers, and I promised to call him if my husband allowed me to trade the house.

As they left, some pressure disappeared. But I still didn't feel comfortable.

The next day I met Milan in front of Merhamet and informed him that Husein wasn't ready to trade houses. All the happiness disappeared from his face. "Talk to your husband again, and explain that a soldier can destroy your house, take all your property, and push you out at any time," he asserted in a demanding voice.

For two weeks I had no visits from soldiers and no late night telephone calls, but the silence wasn't peaceful. I couldn't relax, wondering what the next dawn would bring with its light. The peaceful life was far away. I bought wood for the winter, and Samir and I stored it on the back balcony. The wood was heavy, and I was concerned that the balcony might collapse.

On the first Wednesday in September, the weather, except for a cool morning, was very summer-like. I was busy all day working in the yard. As the sun slowly sank in the west, I completed my day's work by placing red pepper, onion, cabbage, and tomato seeds in marked paper bags, wondering as I worked who would be planting them in the spring.

As night covered the town with its dark blanket, I checked and locked all our doors and windows, and stepped out onto the back balcony to enjoy the twilight and breathe in the fresh evening air. Even the weapons seemed to take a break and allow themselves to be replaced by the soft sound of distant accordion music. As I pushed my hair behind my ears to hear better, I heard a familiar song that brought back happy memories of dances, weddings, and parties. *Ah, those were good times, wonderful memories*, I thought to myself. A new crescent moon was sailing on the sky like a boat on an ocean. The stars glittered, immersing my heart in deep silence.

Is this war helping us draw closer to God, cleansing our hearts and realigning our lives? After contemplating answers, I walked down to the sink, filled a pitcher with fresh water, and returned outside to make ablution. A soft breeze was gently moving the leaves on the nearby apple tree, and the flowers in the garden spread a pleasant scent all around me. I sat on a smooth stone enjoying my beautiful, magic-like surroundings. I prayed to God to forgive my sins and allow me to purify my body and my soul from all wrong things and everything that God does not like. I asked Him to help me be one of His good servants who do not feel fear or sorrow. I thanked Him for the clean water that He granted us, water to drink when we were thirsty and to cleanse our bodies with when we were dirty. I washed my mouth, and I asked God to help me use good words and keep my mouth closed when I needed to listen, reflect, and absorb. I cleaned my nose and asked God to help me to recognize the smell of paradise and protect me from hell's fire. I washed my face and prayed that God would give His light to my face just as He would give it to those dear to Him on the Day of Judgment. Clean drops of water rolled down my right forearm like pearls as I asked God to give me the book of my good deeds in my right hand and help me to pass my test on Judgment Day. I touched my hair with my wet right hand and prayed to God to help me enter paradise with His mercy. When I washed my ears, I asked God to help me be one of His good servants who always would listen to His words and follow them. I touched the back of my neck with my wet hand and prayed that God would free me from hell's fire. I soaked my feet in water and while washing them asked God to forgive my sins. The fresh water cleaned my body, removing the burden from my shoulders. My prayers helped me regain peace in my heart, and I went inside to bed.

At two in the morning a loud explosion shook the house. *Oh, my God! What has happened? Did the whole house collapse? Did Samir and Nana survive? Is another explosion coming? Where should I go?*

An icy fear seized me, chilling me to the very marrow of my bones. In the next instant I heard Samir's voice. *Oh, thank You God, he is alive!* Opening the door, I crawled into his room. He was sitting on his bed in utter shock. His eyes were open, but he was disoriented. I hugged him and helped him to sit on a blanket on the floor. Shards of glass from the bedroom window were still falling from the window frame. "Mom, what happened? Was that thunder or an earthquake? It shook my bed and woke me up." Samir was moving his terrified eyes from the broken glass to my face.

"I don't know. I don't think it was thunder." I paused. "There is no wind or rain," I whispered. A breeze was coming in through the broken window to play with the curtain.

"This room isn't safe," I continued. "Let's move to the hallway." I took Samir's hand, and we walked. Once in the hallway Samir lay down on his blanket.

The idea of checking on Nana stopped my hand from touching her doorknob. *What if she has been killed?* I waited for a minute, opened her bedroom door slightly, and peered inside. Nana lay motionless on her bed. *Is she alive?* My heart pounded. I came closer to her bed and noticed that her yellow and green striped blanket had a shallow but regular up-and-down movement. I let out a sigh of relief. *Sometimes it's good to be deaf,* I thought to myself as I glanced at her unbroken windows.

I couldn't hear our dog. *Oh poor dog. She must be dead.*

I shivered at the thought that a second bomb might be coming. I looked around, but there was nowhere to hide. I picked up the telephone and struggled to dial the police station. I introduced myself and in a trembling voice reported that a bomb or explosive had damaged our house.

I continued, "Three of us are here—"

A policeman's voice interrupted me, "—Wait, wait! Would you feel better if I told you that a Serb house was burned tonight?" he replied and hung up on me.

I couldn't control my fear and anger any more. I threw an empty Coca-Cola bottle through the broken window and another at the wall. I walked to the TV to grab it and throw it, but my brain finally took hold of my anger, and I stopped. "He didn't even ask if there were casualties!" I shouted at no one. "He didn't care if anyone was killed." I gazed through the broken window into the dark, indifferent night. A frightening, deep silence—worse than any sound—chilled me. My head felt as if it were coming apart, and beads of perspiration covered my forehead. My shoulders didn't have any strength, and my heart was pounding so hard that my whole body was trembling. I sat in the hallway close to Samir, pressing my back hard against the wall.

After a few seconds, realizing that my family had survived, I became thankful. *Dear God, thank You for saving my family tonight. Samir was so close. I do not want to imagine the catastrophe that could have happened. All material things are replaceable. Thank you.* My heart softened, and tears accompanied my prayers.

I remembered my neighbor, Ljubica. She had offered to shelter us during the nights. It was three in the morning. I hesitantly called her. Her alert voice surprised me. "Thank you for calling. The explosion woke me up too. I was pretty sure it had come from your house, and I couldn't sleep." She paused. "Don't go outside now. Close all your doors, and wait in your hallway until dawn. Pray! I will pray for you too. I am sure God will answer our prayers and protect your family. There is no change or power except by the will of God."

Her words took about half of my burden away. I sighed thinking how much of a blessing it was to have a good neighbor. With the window broken a moist chill spread through the night, and I covered myself with two warm blankets. Suddenly the barking of our dog moved my heart to beat faster, filling me with happiness. *Our dog is alive! Thank God for saving her.*

I ran upstairs and looked to the east where the sky was turning to pink and gold. The sun rose slowly behind the forests and fields, which still rested in the foggy morning twilight. All the clouds sparkled with astounding light.

I walked through the hallway and opened the front door inch by inch, fearing another explosion. Below me there was an ugly hole in the garage wall. I rubbed my eyes, looked around, and noticed the broken stones and glass in front of the garage and on the steps. I didn't see anything suspicious, so I opened the door wide. The instant the dog saw me she jumped from her doghouse under the balcony, ran to me, and licked my hand, all the while wagging her tail. It was a wonderful embrace.

The garage door was dotted like a strainer with its many holes, and the first and the second floor windows were completely shattered. Looking at all the damage, I shook my head. Just then I heard Ljubica's quick steps. She looked at the hole and declared, "Somebody who wants your house caused this explosion. He wants to save the house but scare you out of it. He could just as easily have destroyed the house and killed all three of you if he had wanted to."

"It must be Milan," I responded. "I am almost sure. He wants our house so badly." The fire of anger inflamed my face. My throat choked, and I became quiet for a second.

Many people came to see me with hugs and tears more beautiful than words. Some of them brought food for my family. Before sunset a few arrived with thick plastic sheets and nails to cover our broken windows. They also helped me clean up the broken glass in and around the house.

The Car

The next day two men showed up at my front door. I was afraid to open it to them, and for a while I observed them through the curtains. A tall slender man with long oily hair dressed in civilian clothes and carrying no visible weapons was pressing the doorbell. He was accompanied by a short, wide-shouldered man with clean black hair. I couldn't see their faces very well. As the tall man pressed the bell repeatedly, I sensed trouble.

I opened the door.

The short man turned his almost rectangular face with deep, dark owl's eyes toward me. He tried to move the corners of his thin lips into a smile and mumbled, "We are looking for—oh, oh, I recognize you. You are Mrs. Softic."

The tall man climbed one of the steps at the front of the house, biting his lower lip. A beard partially covered the yellow skin that stretched tight across the bones of his face. I was shifting my glance from one face to the other in the hope of figuring out who they were and why they had come to my house.

"Mrs. Softic, I don't know how to explain the reason for our visit. It isn't easy to explain, but you'll understand." The short man paused, and his lips danced into a smile. "You know the war is going on. You can imagine soldiers' lives. We are safe here with our families while they are defending us in a war zone." He paused. "Our soldiers need cars to come home to visit their families. The army has ordered us to take your car for their needs. Is your car in the garage?"

I thought of Petar Kocic, a Bosnian satirist who wrote the play, *David Shtrbac*. In the play the police came several times to collect excessive taxes from David, a poor farmer. Because David could not pay, each time the police came they took one of David's animals, beginning with his valuable cow. Each time David thanked

177

the "merciful emperor" for relieving him of the burden of caring for the animals. Now I was about to lose my car, and suddenly I felt like David, but I wisely held my tongue.

Oh, I suddenly realized from the midst of my musing, *I have to answer that question,* "Yes, the car is in the garage."

"Give us the key. We will write a document that we took your car," explained the tall man.

"I'll give you the key, but I'll need to keep the car battery. We connect the battery to our radio, so that we can hear the news. Bring another battery and take the car," I responded politely.

"What are you saying? Are you joking with us? Do you want me to destroy your entire house and show you how we make jokes?" The tall man screamed crazily, violating my personal space. "Your husband is off fighting Serbs in Sarajevo or Zenica, and you are joking with us, with our army?"

I took a few steps back, and the short man came between us. "Wait, wait, both of you wait!" He faced his friend, stating, "Mrs. Softic didn't mean to keep the battery. We cannot drive the car without the battery. She knows that."

Suddenly he returned to me, explaining, "Mrs. Softic, my friend came from the war zone last night. He wanted to come alone to take your car. He is tired and cannot control himself. That is why I came with him. I don't want to see anything bad happen here. We don't need that. You are a smart lady, and you understand the situation here."

"Let me show her," the tall man shouted. "She is like a turkey gobbling in a big house. My parents live in a basement. She is playing games with the battery. She must get off Serb territory! She must go where the other *balijas* are!" The tall man screamed out again.

"Mrs. Softic, give us the key and the battery. I don't know how long I will be able to restrain this man. I told you..." he stated, making the sign for a crazy man and tilting his head and eyes to indicate his tall companion.

I grabbed the key and the battery from the room and handed them over. The tall man, moving a cigarette from his shaking hand to his thick lips, grabbed the battery and took the key. I heard their voices for a few minutes and then the sound of the engine roared. The car slowly backed out of the garage, turned onto the street, and disappeared.

The empty garage seemed horrible with scary darkness inside.

The New Challenge

The explosion and the angry men who took our car destroyed any peace I had found. I felt like a frightened, wounded doe unable to leave my dear forest but scared of the wolves around me. For several nights after the explosion, I couldn't rest or find a safe place to sleep. I switched rooms with Samir. Every time a breeze moved the plastic covering on the window, my heart pounded so hard, and all my body sweated. I understood that the bomb was a sign for me to leave my home. Before dawn, after a sleepless night, I made the final decision. I was going to gather the necessary documents for the three of us and leave our beloved homeland.

In a week, I had half of the documents I needed in my pocket. Nana was also preparing for the journey. She had tied her clothes in one suitcase and polished Husein's shoes that she planned to wear in our travels.

Samir spent all of his free time with his animals. He taught his dog new tricks and let his pigeons alight on his shoulders.

One night near the end of the September, I heard Nana pacing. I assumed that she was still packing even though we had a whole week in front of us to do so. At dawn she called out to me. "I am sick. The pain in my stomach is killing me. I made a big mess," she whispered.

I lit a candle and found Nana, sitting on her bed, her face pale, pressing her belly with both hands. As I brought a mug with steaming tea, I noticed the black line on the rug and on the floor from her bed to the bathroom. It looked like ground coffee.

"I am sorry for the mess, but I couldn't stop myself," she explained, looking at the line.

"Don't worry. I will find a doctor for you." I glanced at her hands, wrinkled and withered now like dry apples. I remembered how hard those hands had worked serving others throughout her long life.

"Only God knows how much I hate to go from this house," she remarked, "but I even got my shoes ready. I don't know what we should do now." The mug in her hands was shaking.

"Nana, we are going to help each other as we always do. We will go through everything that is in front of us together," I assured her, softly touching her hand.

"God bless you, my daughter! God gave you a soft and good heart. I hope He will give you a good life and grant you paradise in the hereafter." A few tears rolled down her cheeks. I cleaned the black trail and gave Nana a bath. When she was in her bed, I called Dr. Ines Todic and explained Nana's problems.

"I don't need to come and see Nana," she replied. "She needs to go to the hospital."

Going to the hospital where my husband had worked was a nightmare for me. With our car now gone, the lack of transportation hit me like a hammer.

I went to the hospital and met the vocational instructor. He transported Nana to the hospital. Doctor Lisica kept Nana in the hospital for three days. The first day the nurse inserted a catheter, but Nana still didn't use the bathroom. When I visited her, she whispered, "Please take me home as soon as possible! The nurses don't help me to go to the bathroom. They told me to pee in my pants. How can an old woman pee in her pants?" she opened her brown eyes wide. Her face was troubled.

"Nana, a nurse connected your bladder to a plastic bag under your bed. Your urine goes in the bag, and you don't need to go to a bathroom. You are fine," I explained to her.

"Nobody told me that," Nana replied, lowering her voice.

The second day was a sad one. The tests showed that Nana had colon cancer. The doctors didn't recommend surgery and suggested that she go home.

"Does Nana need a special diet?" I asked, holding back my tears.

"No, she can eat whatever she wants, but she cannot use the bathroom purposefully any more. The cancer is pressing on the colon, and Nana cannot feel when she needs to go," the doctor explained.

When Nana came home, she shared her hospital experiences. "Oh my dear neighbor, Ilinka, the nurses didn't respect my gray hair.

They need to come to Aisa to learn how to treat an old person. Look at Aisa. Allah made her from gold. Yes, Allah made her from pure gold!" Nana's eyes glowed.

"You are lucky to have her," Ilinka replied, smiling.

"Yes, I am very lucky. She not only serves me well but also talks to me in a soft, respectful voice. I have a big family, and she welcomes everybody at any time. I am thankful to God that Aisa is my daughter-in-law. I don't ask for anything else."

Pleasure filled my heart listening to Nana and Ilinka.

Nana was able to use the bathroom for only a few days. Nobody sold diapers for adults in our town, so I made them from Nana's old clothes. I had a washing machine, but the shortage of electricity made it impossible for me to use it. Every day I fired up the wood-burning stove in the kitchen and boiled the dirty clothes with a detergent. I was glad when the clothes could dry outside during warm, sunny days.

I could see Nana sinking a little bit each day. By the middle of October she was in terrible pain and couldn't find a comfortable position in her bed. Every four or five minutes Nana asked me to move her to the pillows on the floor or switch places with me.

"This place isn't good for me. Please help me return to my place," Nana begged. "Ah, when my son went to medical school, I worked hard and gave him all of my money. I hoped that he'd help me when I got sick. Look at me today! Look at our tragedy!" Nana sobbed. "Please, take me to Banja Luka. They have bigger hospitals and better doctors there."

"I am sorry, but I have no car," I told her softly.

"Oh my dear daughter. Pain is the worst enemy. I have a stabbing pain in my entire belly. Dear God, take me and save me from this suffering." Her painful facial expressions and loud screaming broke my heart.

Around four in the morning I became dizzy, so I awakened Samir to replace me. I went back to Samir's still warm bed and slept for about two hours.

After two days I went to the hospital where the doctor gave me morphine for Nana. I couldn't thank Nurse Fatima enough for her help. She came every night to give Nana a shot. The pain would disappear, and Nana was fine for two or three hours, sitting up, talking, praying, and even sleeping a bit. But each night, just as I was falling asleep, Nana's pain returned, and she would wake me up.

At the end of two weeks of caring for Nana, I was completely exhausted. When our neighbors, Seka and Habiba, saw my tired, yellow face and half-closed eyes, they offered their assistance. Habiba began coming with her children every other night to take care of Nana, which gave me several straight hours of sleep and some of my energy returned. Seka took care of Nana, and I returned to work at Merhamet.

Now we were better organized, but Nana's life was still a life of pain. One morning crying during my prayer, I asked God to help her. The next day we received an answer—Doctor Tendzeric supplied us with Haldol. Nana started to take one tablet each night, and for the first time in two months, she could sleep through the night.

The war companions: Samir, Nana, and me in Bosnia in 1993

Chapter 9—**Difficulties**

Difficulties strengthen the mind, as labor does the body.

—Seneca

The Unforgettable Trip

When it got to be three years since I had seen Aida, my teenage daughter, the wish to see her was greater than any obstacle in my way. For her winter break in 1994 she flew to Germany to visit her aunt in hopes I could find a way for us to meet. I planned to go to Zagreb in Croatia with Merhamet, but I had missed the list approval deadline, and my trip to Zagreb was impossible.

My friend, Habiba, encouraged me to find a solution. "Can you borrow an ID card from one of your Serb friends and travel to Belgrade to see your daughter?"

"What if the police notice that the ID card isn't mine?" I was scared.

"They only read the names; and if a person has a Serbian name, there is no problem," said Habiba. "But, for safety reasons, perhaps you could find someone who looks like you."

"There is a lady who works in the hospital who is about my age with green eyes and curly light brown hair. She told me that some people have called her "Mrs. Softic," but I don't know her very well. I don't even know her name." I paused. "I am not sure that she will help me."

Seka came in and joined our conversation. "You have nothing to lose if you ask her."

Throughout the evening, I contemplated using a fake ID card. One moment I saw myself getting caught at the border, frightened to death as the police handcuffed me and took me off to jail. The next moment in my mind I was crossing the border, and, for the first time in three long years, I spotted Aida's beautiful face and sparkling blue eyes, and, calling her name, I felt the hills reverberate to the sound of my voice. My heart tightened with a mixture of anger and sadness that my name, the present my parents had given me that I had always been proud of, had become a wall separating me from my beloved daughter.

I walked toward the hospital, hunching inside my coat against the snow and cold, and found myself deep in thought about the ID card and how I would make my request. I quietly knocked on the lady's office door and a great block of ice settled in my stomach.

The lady opened her eyes wide. "Oh Mrs. Softic, how can I help you?"

It was the perfect question. Glad that she was alone, I took a deep breath and said almost in a whisper, "I came to ask you to lend me your ID card."

She frowned, and I understood that she needed to know all the details. So, taking courage, I continued, "My daughter came to Germany from the United States. I haven't seen her in three years. You know that I am Muslim and cannot travel anywhere. If I have your ID card, I'll be able to travel to Belgrade." I looked deeply into her eyes.

She sat very quietly, and by the look on her face, I concluded that my words had not softened her heart.

"I will be going alone," I continued rapidly, my hope fading, "I will be leaving my son and my mother-in-law in our home. I will spend only two days with her. That is it."

I looked at what was left of my hope, but her face had turned to stone. I knew that I had asked a great deal, but a mother's heart was heedless, seeking only the small laminated plastic card that would open the way to bring me endless happiness.

"Why are you asking me? Don't you have any friends who can help you?"

"You and I have physical similarities. My chances of passing the border are greater with your picture."

"It is a very sensitive issue. I will have to talk to my husband." She looked at her papers.

"It is very sensitive, yes." I was desperately searching for a way to soften her heart. "If you were in my shoes, I would do it for you." I paused. "I don't have any legal way to travel and meet my child. I am Muslim, a prisoner in my own home." I was ready to cry. "Our religious differences do not matter. We are mothers, and only we know how much we love our children. If someone told me I had to walk on hot coals the entire two hundred and fifty kilometers to

Belgrade to see my daughter, I would do it without hesitation." My tears prevented any further discussion, and I walked toward the door.

"I'll inform you tomorrow what my husband decides."

I knew that the woman was going to turn me down, but I returned to her office to hear the words from her own mouth. She immediately began shouting at me, "My husband is surprised that you could think about committing such a crime and involving me in your conspiracy. How dare you come to me with this request! Using a false ID card is a criminal act." I closed her door, feeling like a hungry child caught attempting to steal a slice of bread.

I walked home in tears and with a broken heart. *My child came from Dayton, Ohio to Frankfurt, Germany. She is ready to come from Frankfurt to Belgrade, but I cannot travel two hundred and fifty kilometers from Bosanska Gradiska to Belgrade. Dear God, help me to see her sky-blue eyes, squeeze her in my hug, touch her hair, and hear her voice. Those feelings are dearer to me than any material things on the earth.*

At home Habiba surprised me with the neighborhood information that I could obtain a legal document from the police that would allow me to travel to Belgrade with my own ID card. I looked at her suspiciously, but she urged me to go to the police station and find out.

I went to the police station at seven o'clock the next morning and asked the policeman at the information desk how I could obtain the travel document that Habiba had described to me.

"You need a document saying that a Muslim woman can travel through the Serbs' Republic to Serbia?"

I nodded.

"I don't know if that is possible." He looked at me as if I had come from another planet.

"Could I talk to the chief of police? He must know if it is possible."

He shook his head but gave me the chief's office number.

I knocked on the door that matched the number and told the secretary who I was and why I had come. She narrowed her eyes and in a firm voice told me to wait in the hallway until the chief was available. I waited for about two hours. Other people went into the office for a few minutes and then left, apparently having been successful with their requests.

When I entered the office at eleven o'clock, the secretary yelled at me, "The chief is not available for you!"

"Other people were coming in, and I thought it must be my turn," I mumbled.

"Your turn is when I tell you. You have to respect rules!" she screamed. I returned back to the hallway like a dog prevented from reaching his food dish.

What kind of "rules" do I have to respect? Muslims don't have any rights in the country where we and our ancestors were born. We are like dust on the floor. Our rights are being robbed, raped, forced from our homes, and even killed. Tears filled my eyes.

I paced in the hallway and prayed to God for self-discipline to control my reaction. After two o'clock, I felt only bitterness in my mouth. The chief appeared in the hallway in his winter coat with his briefcase in hand and walked straight toward me. "My secretary is writing the document for you. Good luck!"

"Wait, please wait," I walked behind him. "You mean, I can travel to Belgrade?"

"The secretary knows the information." The sound of his shoes covered his words.

The secretary opened the door and gave me a signed and sealed paper with written permission to travel to Belgrade. She smiled like she was joking with me or she knew that something creepy was enclosed in the envelope.

"I need to buy a travel ticket for my trip. Do you think that I can do it?" I inquired, puzzled.

"It's your life, so do whatever you want," she responded, bossily.

I went straight to the bus station and bought a ticket on the first bus from Bosanska Gradiska to Belgrade. On my way home I stopped at Ljubica's house and informed her about the trip. She suggested that I hold off telling Aida to come until I had gotten across the Serbian border. She took a piece of paper and wrote down a phone number. "Slavica, my husband's niece, runs a restaurant in Bjeljina. Here is her number. In case you don't pass the border, find her. Mihailo will call her."

I informed Aida that I had the necessary travel document in my purse but suggested she wait to buy her travel ticket until I had gotten across the border."

Nana took something covered in a magazine from beneath her pillow and gave it to me. "This towel is a gift for Aida. Tell her to use the towel to dry her hands before her prayers and to remember her Nana. Please ask her to take good care of my Husein, and give her my *salaams*." Several tears rolled down Nana's face, and she moved her shoes. "Take my shoes because you'll need to walk a long distance. You can wear wool socks to keep your feet warm."

Habiba and Seka promised to be with Nana and Samir and take good care of them.

The entire night mixed feelings occupied my heart, just as they had the previous evening. Those emotions were tearing at my heart and were almost too much to bear. I walked through the rooms of my home, asking God to protect me and my daughter on our trip and to keep the rest of my family safe while I was gone.

I left my home when the first roosters' announced dawn. The cold of the frigid December morning, combined with the thoughts of the upcoming trip, seemed to tighten the very flow of my blood.

The bus arrived on time. As we passed the town of Derventa, the war showed its devastation. The empty villages and destroyed houses sat on both sides of the road. I sighed and wiped my tears. A few dogs were scavenging through debris, and an oak tree hosted several crows.

Suddenly the bus stopped. Soldiers crowded on board, filling every empty seat and the aisle. The entire bus now smelled like a pub. I crouched against my window making myself as small as possible. I looked at my book but couldn't read even a sentence. After about seven hours of riding, the bus finally stopped, and the driver announced a thirty-minute break. The other passengers went into the restaurant, but I walked off a little way to be alone with my thoughts.

The lady who had sat beside me on the bus joined me. "We are almost in Serbia." She came closer to me and asked softly, "Are you Muslim?"

Her question surprised me. My heart skipped a beat, and I found myself unable to speak. I waited a little, looked around, and half-whispered, "Yes, I am Muslim."

"I assumed." She smiled. "As the soldiers entered the bus, your hands trembled and when we passed all those destroyed villages, I noticed tears in your eyes."

We were quiet for a moment.

"I trusted the news reports broadcast in Serbia that the Muslims in Bosnia were causing all the trouble for themselves in order to gain the world's attention. Then I spent ten days in the Serb's Republic, and what I saw changed my mind." She looked at the frozen grass in front of her. "During those days I was ashamed of what the Serb soldiers were doing."

"I cannot think about this dark past right now," I responded. "I have a document from our police, but I am not sure that the police will let me pass the checkpoint." My empty stomach growled with a stabbing pain. I doubled over unable to move. My newfound friend offered help, but I motioned for her to return to the bus. My pain subsided a bit, and I followed the passengers.

After about forty minutes, the driver stopped the bus, opened the door, and two policemen came in.

"ID cards please," announced one of them and began to look at the cards on my side of the bus. I pulled out my ID card and the special Muslim travel document with my trembling hands. Everybody was quiet until he looked at my card. "You are Aisa Softic!" He gazed down at me. "Go to the office!" His strong, bull-like voice paralyzed me. I couldn't move.

"I have the d-d-document. You d-d-didn't see it," I stuttered.

"Go to the office! Did you hear me?" The policeman frowned.

I stood but couldn't stop my legs from shaking. I put my coat on my shoulders, picked up my bag and purse, and headed slowly toward the bus door. As I was passing the driver, he asked me, "Did you take all your belongings with you?"

I nodded and left the bus alone. As the policemen stepped down, the bus began to move away. The distance between me and the bus became larger and larger until the bus passed the checkpoint and crossed the river Drina into Serbia. When the bus disappeared, my hope and excitement at the possibility of seeing my daughter vanished. I was standing and staring as if in a bad dream.

"Why are you standing like a statue? Move! Another bus is coming!" a policeman yelled.

"I thought that our Republic was clean now. But look. Some Muslims still persist! How do you dare come here? Look at where you came from! What do you want?"

My legs were quaking, and I could barely remain standing. "I want to go to Belgrade. I have a document from our police," I tried to explain, placing the paper on the desk in front of him.

He took my document, crumpled it, and threw it in the trashcan.

"I waited for that paper an entire day! I only want to see my daughter!" I was hardly able to contain my anger and pain, but I did not feel fear anymore.

The older policeman came over to me. "Go to Bjeljina police tomorrow. They need to call us and announce that you are coming with their permission."

I sighed again, dried my face, and left the office. The sun had disappeared, leaving a gentle ribbon of light on the horizon. The bridge over the Drina River looked cold, sad, and distant. The river's other side was so close, a few minutes walking distance, but in this war-torn part of the world, it was so very, very far. A cold breeze chilled my face and brought the sad sound of the flowing Drina River to my ears, a sound of crying. My eyes filled with tears. *Cry, my favorite river. Cry, my beloved country! My heart is crying too. I desire for you, my precious river, to flow peacefully and that the bridges above your water connect your banks and your people. I wish for you, my beloved country, to be a safe place for all Bosnians who want to live here.*

I dried my face, came close to a young lady who held a baby, and asked how I could find a bus to Bjeljina. She moved the child to her other arm and invited me to wait for a bus with her. My eyes grew moist with gratitude when the woman promised to help me to find Slavica. The chains around me broke, and I breathed easily.

I thanked her from the bottom of my heart and walked to Slavica's restaurant. A half-moon, slipping in and out from behind scattered clouds, was my new companion. The blowing wind brought the sound of rifles, and I shivered. A group of men with Chetnik symbols appeared on the other side of the street, freezing the blood in my veins. I turned my head down into my coat as much as possible when they passed me.

A middle-aged woman was standing in front of the restaurant. "My uncle asked me twice about you already. I didn't knowing what was going on. Come in." She opened the restaurant door and found a seat for me. After a few minutes she came back carrying a big tray with steaming food.

As I finished the soup, two older ladies joined me. I offered to share the food with them, but they surprised me with their request.

"A small glass of *sljivovica* (plum brandy) would warm me this cold night," explained the one in the fur hat.

"*Sljivovica* is fine for me too," remarked the other lady.

I just stared at them. As a Muslim, I cannot drink, buy, or serve alcohol.

The lady in the fur opened her purse and pulled out a bunch of cards. "Are you a member of any of our patriotic organizations?"

I put a bite of food in my mouth to make myself unable to answer.

"We are very active these days in the fight for our freedom. It is time for all Serbs to live in one country. Only harmony will save the Serbian nation. I am serving Zeljko Raznjatovic, Arkan's soldiers. This card is proof of my membership."

The other lady showed her cards. "This one is evidence of helping Vojislav Seselj's followers. I also advocate for Vuk Drashkovic's movement. Look at these documents!"

The food I had started to swallow stuck in my throat, and suddenly I felt like a mouse in front of two large hungry cats. All three of the organizations were among the most radical of Serbian organizations and among the cruelest to their Muslim enemies.

Slavica's voice freed me. "Ladies, leave my guest alone. Take another table please. She needs to finish her supper, and I need her help in the kitchen."

"Oh, we didn't know she is your guest. Is she your guest? We only talked to her about our work as freedom fighters."

"You are *sljivovica* fighters. I'll bring your drinks, and you can go," responded Slavica, taking my tray and giving me a signal to follow her. She found a chair in her kitchen and let me finish my meal. She shared her secrets about how she was helping and protecting her Muslim friends and neighbors.

When she was ready to leave me in the bedroom in her home, I asked, "What do you think about my chance of crossing the border tomorrow?"

"Honestly, you have a very small chance." She promised to wake me up in the morning and give me directions to the police station.

Waiting at the station, I found a newspaper and read that the former American President Ronald Regan had been diagnosed with Alzheimer's disease. The man who was able to lead the strongest and richest country in the world was becoming forgetful. Diseases attack kings just as they attack every other human being. People need to fight diseases, not each other.

I was surprised that the policeman at the station treated me kindly.

"I am going to write the document for you. You can go and buy a ticket, and I will make a call to the checkpoint," the policeman told me.

I called Aida. "It looks like this time I will be able to get across the border to see you."

"That is wonderful. I am going to buy a ticket as well."

Slavica was astonished that the policeman wrote the document for me. "You are very lucky. I did not think the police would be willing to help a Muslim in any way. But we never know." She stared at my document.

As the bus came to the checkpoint, I handed a policeman my ID card and the document without fear. When he opened his big mouth, I thought he was screaming at some other unfortunate Muslim who was without the proper document from Bjeljina's police.

"Are you deaf? Can you hear me?" he asked me angrily.

"I have a document from Bjeljina's police," I stated, handing him my authorization.

"You are crazy, woman! Go out!" he screamed, shaking his head.

I stood up, speechless, stepped off the bus with as much dignity as my surprise and anger would permit, and strode quickly to the office.

"There is a mistake here," I protested to the border officer. "I obtained a travel permit from the Bjeljina police just a few hours ago, and the officer promised he would notify you."

"You cannot pass the border! You must go back!"

The room began to spin, and I walked somewhat unsteadily outside into the cold. I gritted my teeth and kept my mouth shut. *How can policemen be so cruel? Why are they playing with me? Are they happy doing this? Don't they realize that someday, they will be asked to account for how they treated me and other people?*

I found out that the next bus to Bjeljina was leaving at five o'clock. That meant I would not be able to get to a phone in time to call to Aida. I must tell her about my problems. I walked toward a driver in a black Mercedes and asked him if I could go with them to Bjeljina. As I sat down, the lady in the front seat asked me, "Why are you in such hurry?"

I couldn't hold in my anger and frustration any longer. "Serbs are treating us as the Nazis treated the Jews." I covered my face with my hands and let the tears run. "I couldn't pass the border the second time," I mumbled.

When I finally reached Aida by phone, I only sobbed.

"I am sorry for all of your troubles, but you did all that was in your power to make our meeting possible. It looks like God has a different plan for us. Don't be sad. If it is God's will, we will see each other again soon." Aida's gentle words were calming, giving me some relief.

When Slavica saw me and my red eyes, she assured me, "This difficult time will someday be only as a bad dream." She patted my shoulder. "Go visit my Muslim neighbors, Muris and his wife. When I finish my work, I'll come there too." She smiled, but I was unable to smile back.

Just as I got there, I greeted a lady in long dress and a warm vest with *Asselamu Alejkum*, assuming she must be Muris's wife. She turned her head and walked up the outside stairway to the second floor.

"I am looking for Muris and his wife. Is this their house?"

"They live on the first floor," she answered from the highest step.

Muris and his wife welcomed me warmly. Their gray hair and wrinkled hands and faces revealed their age, and their eyes could not hide their sadness. Muris, touching his lips with his index finger, gave the quiet sign and whispered that a Serbian family had taken over their second floor.

After a few minutes, the room looked like a nursing home. Every one of them had a similar war story, and all talked at the same time, making the room hum like a beehive. I listened quietly. One lady asked me why I had come to Bjeljina. The question quieted the room, and I spoke my story. They asked many questions about my daughter. Once I described my experience at the border, I broke down sobbing. Many of them dried their own tears. Muris shrugged his shoulders hopelessly. His wife moved closer to me and with deep compassion patted my hands. Sighing, I raised my head and told them that I would have to trust in God to see my daughter another time and I must to be more patient. How many mothers did not have even that hope?

In the morning I walked out of the city and waited for a bus at a roadside bus stop where I found a large group of people already waiting.

A middle-aged lady in the group came closer to me, "I want to go to Banja Luka, but I haven't been able to catch a bus for the last three days. Some buses haven't stopped at all. Some of them picked up only one or two passengers. They were always men. They use their strength to push women out of their way. I am losing hope of ever getting on the bus."

"I have a sick mother-in-law at home. I cannot wait here that long for a bus." I was positive that I was the only Muslim in the group. *I am stuck here. I cannot go anywhere.*

As a bus was approaching, people were converging from different directions at the bus stop. Strong men and several soldiers pushed me back to the end of the line.

"I am not sure that all of us could fit in the bus even if it were empty," remarked the woman.

Oh my God. It is true. I don't have any chance to make it onto the bus. This bus looks full. How am I going to get home? Dear God, help me.

When the bus door opened, I recognized the driver's face. He looked in my direction and ordered everyone, "Make space for this lady to come onto the bus, please."

Does he mean me? I placed my right hand on my chest as a form of a question.

"Yes, you. You came with us here two days ago. I remember you," he replied.

Many men stepped aside and made way for only me to get on the already full bus. *Oh my God, this is a miracle. Among all those people he chose me, even though he must have known that I am Muslim.*

"Thank you, thank you very much," I told him as I climbed aboard the bus, relieved.

My son, Nana, and my dear friends welcomed me back with open hearts.

"God gave you love for your child," Nana stated. "You did your part. Have patience, my daughter. Look at my life. I delivered seven children, and now there are none here to take care of me. I am not sure that I will ever see any of my six children again." Nana dried her tears.

I thanked God that I came back home safely and had finished my unforgettable trip.

Here is Samir giving Nana some water to drink. This picture was taken in Bosnia in 1993.

Dead Phone

It was a cold February in 1995. I tried to call my sister, but the phone gave no sound. I checked its cord and the plugs at both ends. Everything seemed fine, but the phone was dead. *The telephone worked last night,* I mumbled to myself. *So what is wrong this morning? This cold weather we are having must have damaged the wires.*

Walking over to the window, I looked at the early morning sky, pale blue, almost white, that mirrored in our icy garden. The sun seemed frozen, and its light was weak in the winter cold. A few people were walking down with their clouds of white breath coming out from their hidden faces. *What are they doing in this cold? Are they fixing the wires for our phones?*

I dressed warmly to go to work hoping that the phone problem would be repaired by the time I returned home. I met my neighbor, Mrs. Fetah who was confused, as if she was looking for guidance in a chaotic world. "Is your telephone disconnected? I met Serbs who are disconnecting Muslim's phones," she whispered.

"Disconnecting?" I couldn't comprehend it. "Oh, I thought they were fixing them." I paused. "Yes, my telephone is dead. I checked everything but couldn't seem to figure out why it wasn't working."

"We are cut off from the world, completely vulnerable and unable to call for help," she whispered. Fear and anger covered her face.

The anger and cold had squeezed my skin tight against my bones, and my eyes bulged like ping-pong balls. "My husband and daughter call me every week from the United States. I cannot afford to call them! What should I do now?"

"Maybe people in Merhamet can help you out," Mrs. Fetah replied to me softly.

When I got to Merhamet, all of my co-workers asked, "Is your telephone disconnected?"

I realized that our entire work force was cut off. Everyone in the office was obviously worried. We had all lost hope that this terrible war would end any time soon.

197

Sanela tapped my shoulder, asserting, "You must know somebody in the Government Building, your ex-students or former co-workers. Go there and question, protest—do something! They could help us to reconnect our phones."

"I know Ratko Micanovic, the former teacher from our high school. I am surprised that he holds a position in the ministry in the Serb government. He was aloof, almost antisocial in the school." I shook my head. "I will go and talk to him, but I am not optimistic."

Mr. Bacic, turning his head, expressed, "In this defective society people do not fit their positions—neither personally nor professionally. As Muslims we don't have any legal way to fight for our rights and justice."

I walked to the Government Building recalling my pain when I had fought to save my wheat crop and when I had attempted to travel to see my daughter. My stomach churned, and my heart raced the entire way.

As I entered Mr. Micanovic's office, the stale air stank of cigarette smoke and liquor, making it difficult to breathe. My former colleague sat rigid behind his desk, furrowing his brow as he attempted to manufacture an artificial smile. An antique wooden clock on the wall behind him ticked away the seconds.

He frowned fiercely, when I mentioned the disconnected phones. "Have a seat, Mrs. Softic," he told me. "All my life I have had to listen to the disgusting stories of how the Turk-Muslims treated Serbs. They took Serbs' kids from their mothers and raised them as Muslims. Mehmed Pasha Sokolovich was one of those kids. Can you imagine how Serbs react to the memory of those brutalities?" His eyes revealed hatred and his voice found courage as he spoke. "I swore to God and myself that I'd take revenge, that I will do the same to Muslims as they did to Serbs hundreds of years ago." He kept on talking, but I was no longer able to listen to his words. My mind was spinning, caught in the tornado of his blind hatred.

I felt a shiver in my legs, and I stood up. I had realized that there was no way we were going to be able to have a useful discussion. I had come to him with a specific problem, and he purposely avoided it by immediately launching himself into a hate-filled speech about an injustice that had taken place long before either of us was born. Why should I pay in 1995 the price for what happened hundreds of years ago?

"My mother-in-law is very sick," I explained. "I am not sure how long she will last. We…"

"I cannot help you," he interrupted. "My mother-in-law is Catholic. Her telephone has been disconnected also. Can you imagine how my wife feels?" For a few seconds he moved his lips in a wild, shrieking laugh. "But I can't change anything. I have to follow Serb policies uncompromisingly." He frowned and shouted in a gruff, mannish voice. "I cannot treat you as a former colleague. I think of you as my enemy from hundreds of years ago."

I tried to determine how to bring light to his darkness. I was ready to tell him that angry people try to harm one another and that anger is not healthy, but his telephone rang. He ignored it to finish his ominous lecture. "We don't trust Muslims." He smiled a little bit. But that shadow of a smile disappeared, and his voice became stern. "We have to finish our job. Our republic must be cleansed of Muslims. Because of international pressure we will have to keep two to three percent of the Muslim senior population, but they will die of natural causes in a few years, and then we will be completely clean." There was pride in his voice as he finished.

"What are you talking about?" I asked sharply. "We have to break that cycle. If we continue to plant seeds of hatred, we will continue to harvest the murder and war we see around us now!" I stood up. "Put yourself in my shoes if you want to see my feelings. Hatred is destroying our human personality, pushing us back to the Middle Ages and to this terrible war. All of us must help each other to end this awful war and build bridges of love and humanity. We need to create Bosnia as a country of 'one nation, under God, invisible, with liberty and justice for all.'" I closed his door.

The loss of our telephones was devastating for all of us. But, after several days, people were visiting each other more often, and their conversations and companionship made the breaks between the bombing and shooting less frightening.

At the beginning of March my dear friend Yelena came to my home. Red-faced she told me, "I've being trying to call you for several days, but every time I call, I get a busy signal. Is something wrong with your phone?"

"All Muslims' phones are disconnected."

Her eyes snapped open, wide like an owl's. "Oh God," she leaned her forehead on her palms, "I cannot believe what my people are doing to Muslims. How cruel!"

"I am like an animal trapped in a cage without any opportunity to ask for help." I shared the story of my meeting with Minister Micanovic. I told her of all the fear, hurt, and anger I had suffered in my attempts to see my daughter. Once I started talking, I found myself unable to stop. I also confessed my stupid idea that I could borrow an ID card from someone I hardly knew. Stiff with shame and rage, I refilled Yelena's coffee cup. She listened patiently.

Yelena placed her hand on my shoulder, and suddenly brightness beamed from her eyes. "I can lend you my ID card, so you can travel to see your child," she whispered.

My heart took a leap of joy. Even though I was not sure that I would ever try to arrange a similar trip again, I responded, "We both could get into lots of trouble if somebody recognizes me there." I sighed and shut my eyes, remembering what had happened when I had tried to cross the border.

"I am your friend and am ready to do it for you. I want you and your family to know that I am ashamed of what some Serbs are doing to you."

"Your husband or your grown children could prevent you from lending me the card," I shared with her, remembering the lady that I had asked the favor.

She was silent for a few seconds. "I am responsible for my actions. I don't have to tell him or anybody else about why I would do something like this," she whispered.

The room became quiet. Nana, sleeping in her bed, moved her legs under the blanket. Her shoes, polished and shiny, were on her dresser.

"One day all of our troubles are going to go away," I offered softly. "Look at Nana. She does not need any ID cards, or even shoes for her trip. She will use her own name, her deeds, and leave everything behind."

"It is true. That is a big reason why we need to help each other—to make our travel easier." Walking outside, she stared at the telephone poles and useless telephone wires, shaking her head. I told her how much her true friendship meant to me at this dark time of war.

Empty Shoes

In the second week in March 1995, Nana developed a high fever and could barely open her mouth to swallow a few bites of soft food. On the morning of March 15, she awoke with her eyes only half-open, glanced around the room, and then fell back to sleep. I looked closely at her sallow face and recognized in it the generosity of her soul. As I recalled how she had guided me through my religion and had helped me raise my children, tears rolled down my cheeks.

Suddenly, she partially rose, with eyes closed and sweat dripping from her forehead. "Mother, I am coming. What do you want? What could I bring to you?" Nana inquired of her mother who had died more than half century previously.

Her head touched the pillow again, and she became quiet.

When I came home from work, for a moment I gazed at Nana in utter silence. Her breathing had become shallower, and the time between breaths had lengthened. A sense of unspeakable anxiety saturated my spirit. I tried to wake her, but she didn't respond.

Habiba, entering the room, looked at Nana's face. "Nana is moving away from us to another world. I remember this breathing when my mother was passing away," she confided with tears filling her eyes.

"Let's pray together and ask God to help Nana now," I said.

"Come here," Habiba told me, touching my hand gently. "Nana has stopped breathing." Deep silence filled the room, chilling my skin. "Look—her eyes are still half-opened." Habiba gently pulled Nana's eyelids down, but they would not completely close. "Nana wished to see somebody before she passed away. She couldn't see her children." Habiba, sobbing, covered Nana's body with a white sheet. Mehmed went to talk to the imam about the funeral.

Ljubica offered me the use of her telephone, and I called Husein.

"Sadly Nana has passed away," I told him as the frigid water of sadness rushed through my bloodstream and brain, chilling me like a block of ice. I wished for nothing so much as to be able to be with him and hold him in his hour of overwhelming sadness. "We need be thankful to God that we had Nana in our lives," I went on, wiping my tears and willing my voice to remain steady. "The last three years have been an awakening for me. Nana taught me so much about life. Her words mirrored God's words in the Qur'an, and her actions mirrored her words. She was truly a gift to my life."

"I am sad beyond any way to say it." Husein's words were broken by his sobs. "My dear mother has died, and I cannot come home even to bury her. This is the most difficult day of my life." He sobbed again, and his words drowned in his sorrow.

Twilight had come, and many of our neighbors, their coats pulled high to hide their faces from soldiers, came to our home to express their condolences. Elvira, Mehmed, Ljubica, Mihailo, and Mustafa sat with us for several hours, but our dear neighbors, Seka, Habiba, Esma, Enisa, Meho, and Vasva, stayed the entire night. I prayed to God to reward them for their love and compassion.

It made me uneasy to have Nana's dead body in the house, so that night seemed endless. According to Bosnian Muslim custom, only men could stay in the same room with the deceased. With no sons left in the country, the responsibility fell to young Samir. Fortunately Meho Vrbanjac stayed with Samir the entire night.

Our dear neighbors had a heightened sense of awareness—an extreme sensitivity to every sound and movement around them. When night finally cloaked the town in black, they shared the sad events in the village of Chikule. Whispering softly with darting eyes, they explained that one of the villagers had died and some neighbors and Fata Mehinovic, the sister of the deceased man, had come to spend the night with the family.

Word had gotten around the village of the man's death and had also gotten to the Serb soldiers policing the village. Knowing that the family must have at least 100 German marks saved for the funeral, the soldiers showed up at the house and demanded the money. Fata, realizing the danger everyone was in, explained to the soldiers that her son had joined the Serb army. She thought that this would protect her and the other mourners. But there was no protection in the vicious kind of war that was going on in Bosnia. The only ones who were safe were those who gained Allah's protection. The soldiers simply shot her and left her dead body lying in the doorway.

Upon hearing their chilling story, I prayed, asking God for His protection that night and thanking Him for blessing us with good neighbors who willingly risked their own lives to help our family.

The imam had arranged for Nana's funeral at noon the following day and asked me to get the death certificate before the funeral. I fixed a scarf on my head—a Muslim sign of mourning—and took my purse. I placed my purse on the fence next to the street just long enough to get my bicycle out of the garage. With a hammering pain in my head and bitterness in my mouth, I pedaled my bicycle toward the hospital, forgetting the purse.

I asked the nurse at the front desk for Nana's death certificate.

"We never took care of your mother-in-law, so we cannot give you the death certificate."

Shocked at her response, I inquired, "But the funeral is at noon and the imam needs the document. Where else should I go?"

"Who was the last to take care of her?" asked the nurse.

"She was diagnosed with terminal cancer six months ago in this hospital's internal medicine unit. I am going there." I walked straight up to the floor where my Husein had worked.

The first thing I saw there was Dr. Borisavljevic's face. Remembering how badly he had treated me when I came to pick up Husein's last check, I glanced around, looking for any other doctors. But unfortunately no one else was there, so I approached him.

"Husein's mother died yesterday." I swallowed hard. "We have arranged for her funeral today at noon. I need a document certifying her death before we can proceed. She received her last medical treatment here. Can you please write it for me?"

"No, I cannot write it," he informed me and looked back at his book.

I stood silent for a few seconds, looking at him sullenly. *Hey, doctor, do you have any humanity left in you at all? Your colleague's mother is dead. Husein worked with you for some twenty years. Did you hear me? The imam cannot perform the funeral without a death certificate.* Suddenly, filled with rage, I wanted to scream, to activate the fire alarms, break the windows, and tear down the doors. But instead I channeled the energy into my fists, squeezing them tightly, and thinking as I did so, *I must leave this disgraceful foolishness and ask for Allah's help.*

I gently wiped my tears with my hands and slowly walked down the stairs thinking: *If they send me from one office to another, play games with me as they did at the border, I am going to write my own certificate titled "Nana's and all Muslims' Death Certificate."*

I came back to the front lobby and the same nurse asked, "Did you get it?"

"No, I don't have the document. Dr. Borisavljevic refused to write it." I paused to stop the tears. "Listen, Dr. Softic's mother died yesterday. Dr. Softic was her personal doctor. He is a refugee in America now. I need that document before we can have the funeral..."

"I didn't recognize you in that scarf, Mrs. Softic." She smiled. "You were my teacher in the nursing school. I liked your psychology lessons." She walked toward the door. "We will give you the document. No problem. A doctor will ask you a few questions."

"How much do I need to pay?" Reaching to my side, my hands searched for my purse. *Where did I leave it? All my money is in it!* I looked at the nurse frantically. "I forgot my purse, but I'll bring money right after the funeral."

"There is no charge for the document," she replied.

It took only a few minutes to get the document, which I speedily put in my pocket and then turned to leave.

I left the hospital in tears. *Muslims have many difficulties and challenges not only to live, but to die and get a funeral. Look how many problems I had to obtain this document.* I dried my face. *Oh, where did I leave my purse?* I began to retrace my steps. *I had the purse in my hand when I left home. Purse, purse—I left it on the fence! Yes, I left it on the side of our street—a very busy street.* Suddenly I froze. *Today is Thursday, market day! Hundreds of people will be passing by the fence. I had 500 German Marks in there for Nana's funeral. People are robbing houses and killing each other for even small amounts of money. The purse is surely no longer there. How can I pay the funeral expenses? What can I do now?* My whole body was covered in sweat. Bitterness filled my mouth. I hardly had the energy to peddle the bicycle home.

As I approached, I spotted the purse—still on the fence. *Could this really be my purse?* Almost in disbelief, I opened the purse with trembling hands. The wallet and all the money sat untouched. *This is a miracle!* I thought to myself. *This is a true miracle! So many people passed by, yet nobody saw it. Oh merciful and compassionate God, thank You from the bottom of my heart. You made my purse invisible today. I'll share this miracle with others.*

The miracle gave me satisfaction to welcome people and make room for every person to relax a little bit before the funeral. The imam, Besim Sheper, came around eleven o'clock, and we agreed to bury Nana in the nearest graveyard. Nana had wished to be buried in Orahova, the village she had lived for more than seventy years, but with the war raging, it would be nearly impossible.

By noon our house and yard were full of people. Among them were many neighbors and all of my co-workers from the Merhamet. Their presence and emotional support helped to fill the void of all the people who couldn't be present—Husein and Aida, as well as all her other children and grandchildren. Covered with the green linen fabric that Nana kept for years for this purpose, her body was laid on wooden boards. The men lifted the boards on their shoulders and carried Nana's earthly remains gently to the waiting carriage. I stayed in the yard, watching as the horse slowly drew the carriage toward the graveyard with the men walking in a dignified procession behind. It was, in a way, like watching Nana slowly fade away in the final days of her life.

Through a warm stream of tears, I thought, *Allahemanet, my dear Nana. I am sorry I didn't ask you for forgiveness. I always thought that we had time. I forgive you for everything. Thank you for helping me to become a stronger and better person. Thank you for choosing to live with me over your own daughter. I am sorry that the war prevented you from having the funeral in your Orahova and that your children and grandchildren couldn't come today. I know how much you loved all of them. Samir is going to place your body in your grave today.*

Dear God, please forgive Nana and grant her paradise on Judgment Day. Thank You for giving me the chance during these difficult days to serve Nana. It wasn't easy, but with Your help I was able to do it. Please allow us to see each other in Your paradise. Amen.

The cozy and warm feeling when Nana was present in the house had disappeared.

My brother Munib's wife, Fata, came close to me and whispered, "I am going to stay with you for the first couple of days." After sunset, she, Samir, and I prayed together. I recited the Qur'an and asked God to grant Nana paradise. Her shiny shoes sat on her dresser and told Nana's stories quietly to my empty heart.

I left my purse on the fence and went to the hospital to get Nana's death certificate. I was absent for at least one hour, but nobody touched my purse.

Chapter 10—Perseverance

Let perseverance be your engine and hope your fuel.

—H. Jackson Brown, Jr.

Refugees Occupied My House

Travel was impossible during Nana's illness, but now my resilience to fight for our home and justice were waning, and submission had taken over. The walls stopped echoing Nana's prayers, and my soul became empty Even a light touch of wind on a window or door made me jump in anticipation of who was on the other side. I started to run through the calendar, counting the days remaining in Samir's school year.

Sensing that the first of May would be my last Bosnian celebration Labor Day at home, I made fresh bread dough. As I washed my hands, an ear-piercing explosion knocked me away from the sink. The sound of grenades exploding shook the house over and over again.

Breathing heavily, I ran upstairs, calling, "Habiba, Habiba! Grenades are exploding!"

"I don't know what is going on!" she whispered, almost paralyzed with shock. She covered her face with her hands. "Karadzic said he is dragging Bosnia into hell and the Muslim nation into annihilation. It looks like he is achieving his goals."

At eight o'clock, on the TV the Zagreb channel featured the headline, "CROAT ARMY ATTEMPTING TO FREE SLAVONIA AND REOPEN THE HIGHWAY."

As we looked at each other, Habiba announced, "I am going home to pack our suitcases." She shook her head. "Please send my children home."

I decided to wash clothes to try to lower my anxiety. As I spread the washed clothes on a rope, our neighbor Cvijeta signaled me to come closer.

"I came here to catch my breath. I can't believe what is going on." She sighed. "The Croatian army has the newest European and American weapons. They are killing thousands of Serb civilians and throwing them out of their homes. Croats are on the other side of the Una River only forty kilometers away. They will be at the Sava River very soon."

"What should we do?" I asked surprise.

"Oh poor Serb's civilians," she lamented, clearing her throat. "I hope the Croats are not coming to Bosnia now, but you never know. We are so close to the border." She blinked several times.

"I feel sorry for all the civilians suffering in this war," I remarked, thinking of the many Muslim civilians killed in the war by both Serbs and Croats. Each had made its own concentration camps and torture centers, and each had interned thousands of Muslims.

"I'll be at home all day. If you need my help, please let me know," I offered, picking up my empty laundry baskets and running through my garden to Habiba's house to share the news.

"This fighting isn't good for us. The Serbs will come here from Croatia and push us out from our homes. Go home and pack your suitcase!" Her explanation made sense, but I just didn't want to accept it.

"Why do we need to pay the price for their fights?" I questioned angrily.

On my way home anxiety and fear took over. I went upstairs, collected all the books that had served as hiding places for money, took documents and jewelry, and brought it all downstairs. I was exhausted, but adrenaline prevented me from getting any rest.

A few minutes after three o'clock, a heavy knock on the door scared me. I left some books on the floor and opened the door. A Serb soldier, brandishing his weapons, was on my front steps.

"Mrs. Softic," he stated in a loud, intimidating voice. The people sitting in a truck in the driveway grabbed my attention. "My family and friends are coming to your house." He signaled for the people on the truck to come in. I stood at the door, confused. When all of them had entered, I walked back inside as though I was one of the intruders. My glance caught their gazes, and I was touched by their sadness. Three elderly ladies dried their tears with the corners of their black scarves and sighed deeply. Five young ladies carried children.

I rushed to the kitchen without finishing counting all of them and brought to the table all the food that I had. "The food is ready," I announced, looking at the younger ladies. "Please help yourselves, and feed your children. I am going to make soup, more fresh bread, and a lot of tea. We will have enough food for everybody. Please come to the kitchen, and I'll try to help you."

Two elderly women came into the kitchen. Still crying, they told me that their sons hadn't been able to break through the Croat army line. Being a mother myself and having lived with my very ill mother-in-law when her son, a doctor, hadn't been able to help her in the most critical moment of her life, I felt their emotions. I forgot that they were enemies, and, since they had come to my house, I looked at them and served them as my guests. *There is no true victory in a war. Civilians are paying the price.*

The soldier in uniform was in charge. In the late afternoon more people came to the house without asking my permission. I was continually fixing food for newcomers, and the whole house smelled of fresh baked bread. I did not have time to pay attention to the sound of shooting going on outside. In the twilight, I met the soldier in the hallway, and it appeared that some of the hatred had vanished from his eyes. "Thank you for your help. It was very nice of you, but you really don't need to serve us. We have enough young people here to take care of the children and the old people."

I looked at him, puzzled. *Is he the same soldier? Did my bread change his heart?*

"I am glad to help," I responded. "Let me know if you need more food or blankets."

"We must use your rooms. We need a place to live, and we have no other choice," he explained softly. "You can keep one room downstairs for you and your son." He paused. "Our people are going to use your kitchen. You can cook in your kitchen too."

Just then a strong male voice calling my name interrupted our conversation. I was surprised when I saw my cousin Redjo, his wife, and their six children on the steps.

"We are terrified to stay in our own home tonight," Redjo informed me. "Many Serbs are coming from Croatia, and we are frightened they could come to our home and kill us. May we please sleep here?" Redjo whispered, holding a baby in his hands.

"Yes, of course!" I affirmed, walking towards the kitchen. "Thank God we have enough space in the kitchen for your family." I had two sofas and several blankets for Redjo's family.

"We have many guests tonight." I did not mention who they were.

When Seka, Habiba, and her children came to our room, we locked the door and made places to sleep. Samir and Muhamed, Habiba's son, slept on the sofas, but Habiba, her daughter Aldiana, Seka, and I sat close to each other and listened carefully to all the sounds in and around the house.

"How many people are in the house?" Seka asked softly.

"More than thirty," I whispered.

"I'm frightened," Habiba shared, "frightened that they may come upon us in the night and kill us all. Some of them looked very angry."

"I am not sure that we are safe in this house anymore," uttered Seka as she pulled the coffee table closer to the door.

"It is good that Redjo came with his family here," I answered softly. "The Serbs don't know who he is, and they may think he is our protector."

Around midnight all sounds ceased. Habiba and I shared our fearful thoughts until the roosters announced the coming of a new day. I walked through the house, silent as a shadow, and made myself ready for prayer.

When Redjo recognized the people in the kitchen, he jumped up as though a hornet had stung him, signaled his older boys, grabbed the hands of his young children, and ran outside. I followed them carrying a basket with bread and sour cream. Once outside Redjo's wife and I spread sour cream on dinner rolls and gave them to the children who were still half asleep.

"Why didn't you warn me who your guests are?" Redjo protested.

"Thank God, we survived," his wife added as they walked home.

The kitchen became a beehive. I showed the ladies how to mix powder and water to make milk and where the tea herbs, coffee, and sugar were. When I began making another ball of bread dough, the elderly lady came close to me and touched the dough. "Thank you for making bread. Everyone likes it."

"If we have bread, we cannot go hungry," I told her, still kneading the dough. "Look, Monday, May 8, is a holiday for me. I am Muslim, and I celebrate Eid. I'll make pitas for all of us that day."

"Are you really Muslim?" she whispered, and our eyes met. I didn't understand what she wanted to know. She noticed my confusion and then clarified, "Your mother, father, husband, and children are Muslims too?"

"Yes, we are all Muslims," I answered washing my hands.

"I've never met Muslims before. I thought that Muslims were different—dirty, unfriendly, ignorant—that they were all our enemies. I didn't want to come here yesterday, and I especially didn't want to end up spending the night with Muslims." She became quiet for a moment. "But your hospitality and generosity have surprised me." The tone of her voice sounded like an apology.

I surveyed the area with a few quick glances and whispered, "God is one. He created Adam and Eve. All of us are their children, one family with similar souls and bodies. We are born with different talents and different abilities, and we are divided into different religions, races, and groups in order to help and learn from each other. It is people who breed pride and hatred, spread misunderstanding and even blood on this earth in the name of religion, ethnicity, culture, or tradition. But every one of us has to return to God and answer to Him about our deeds and doings on this earth."

"You are right," she affirmed with a gentle smile.

After lunch a strange mix of screaming, crying, and laughter was sounding from upstairs. I ran to the hallway and heard, "Mr. Golic just came back from Croatia. His family and friends are shouting and crying for joy."

Not wanting to disturb their celebration, I went back to my room. The older lady opened the door, and the soft glow in her eyes touched my heart.

"Thank God, my son came." She paused. "We are leaving your house now, and I want to thank you for everything you did for me and all of our families." She opened her old arms and embraced me.

"I am only sorry that we had to meet under these terrible circumstances," added a strong voice coming from a tall, middle-aged, exhausted officer. He sat on the steps, covering his face with his hands. "Oh, Mrs. Softic, our leaders, Serb leaders, betrayed us." He sobbed. "At the beginning of the war they gave us weapons and instructed us to resist Croatian politics. They promised to support us to build Serbs' Krajina. Yesterday they left us to defend ourselves! This is a great shame!" Tears rolled down his cheeks.

I was quiet, uncertain of what to say.

"Western Europe, especially Germany, that old bitch, is helping the Croats. They've given them the best weapons. Many Serbs were killed yesterday." He stood up and pointed with his finger. "I am going to Banja Luka to kill Croat families and take their homes. Their soldiers pushed me from my home yesterday, and that is what I will do to them." He paused. "Thank you for taking care of my family."

Life in Risk

After a few days I began to feel as if I were running a hotel for pilgrims. So many people shifted in and out each day, and it was impossible to keep track who was arriving and who was leaving. I was still fine with the women and children, but I didn't trust the men and avoided them whenever possible. My house became tense, devoid of any peace.

Finally, I wasn't able to handle the disorganized confusion any longer, and I went to see Yelena. As I shared all my worries, she promised to come by later in the day to assess the danger.

I just finished preparing spinach pita when Yelena entered with her son, Sasha. She took only a few bites, left her plate, and declared, "I'll go to the living room to see what is going on there. I'll be back soon." Yelena walked quietly to the room, closing the door behind her.

Sasha shared his plan of going somewhere to devote his life to God. We had just begun our conversation when Yelena came back with a worried look on her face.

"Aisa, you are not safe here. You have to go from this house as soon as possible."

"Why? I've been treating them with respect and dignity and have been sharing my home and my food with them. We're only using one room in the entire house," I whispered coming closer to Yelena.

"Even this room is no longer safe for you. Leave now! Do not stay here even a single night longer!" Her lips became tight.

"It is impossible. I don't know when the bridge will reopen."

"I'll give you my ID card, so you can go to Serbia. It could be dangerous, but staying here is worse. Believe me. It is worse. You have a fifty percent chance of saving your life and Samir's if you flee to Serbia. But if the two of you stay here in this house, you will almost certainly die. Think about it!" Yelena firmly stated, but in a low tone. She closed her eyes and frowned. "Come to my home; don't sleep in your house tonight," she urged with finality, and they left.

I found two gallon-containers and planned to go to my sister when I met Seka in the hallway.

"I am going to Dubrave to get milk for us. I'll be back before dark."

"I'll rest here. Ride safely."

As I pedaled toward my sister's home, I noticed the elementary school I had attended so many years before, and a memory floated back to the day I had enrolled in the first grade. I almost heard Mother's words again, "Follow this path, and it will lead you to the school. You cannot miss it. I know you can do it."

I had indeed followed the path much further than my mother ever expected I would, and the memories of those years filled my eyes with so many tears that I had trouble standing on my bicycle. "Oh my dear mother," I said aloud. "I cannot see the path, and I don't know where I need to go. I am searching for the right path not only for me but for my son too. I love him more than I love myself." Drying my tears, I prayed, *Dear God, open a good path for my son and me and protect us. You are the great protector.*

When Dervish saw traces of tears in my eyes and heard about Yelena's suggestions in my trembling voice, she frowned. "It is too dangerous for you to travel by bus." She became quiet, but her eyes moved as if she were making a plan. "My daughter, Esma, and her husband, Hamdija, have friends in Belgrade; maybe they can help you. With two Serbs in the car your documents would be less likely to be questioned. I'll call Esma and see what they can do."

My throat tightened, and I couldn't talk. While Dervisha walked to our brother's house to ask some Serbs there to use their phone, I meandered behind her house, hiding under an apple tree. The land under my feet was too hard, and the sky above me was too high. I prayed, *Dear God, I am begging You to send good people now to help me to travel safely from this place and guide my son and me to join my husband and my daughter.*

Dervisha came back smiling. "Esma informed me that their friends were coming on Friday after work to visit us and returning to Belgrade on Sunday. She is positive that they will help you.

I took the gallons of milk with mixed emotions—excited that such a respectable response from Belgrade had come so quickly and scared of the trip with the false documents. Even with the spring's gorgeous flowers and renewed green grass, my village looked somehow gloomy, empty, and frightened.

My home appeared in the distance, but I found myself afraid to return. When I opened the door, Seka, looking white as a sheet, grabbed my arm and pulled me into the room. Closing the door quietly behind her, she faced me and, with her hand partially covering her mouth, whispered almost hysterically, "Oh my God, I heard them! The door was open, and I heard every word. One of them was yelling that he was going to stay here in your house and that he was going to 'take care of you—good care!' He laughed maniacally as he mentioned your name."

"Go ask Habiba if we can sleep at her house tonight," I responded, holding her hands.

I went to the kitchen. The women were fixing supper, and the men were sitting around. Everyone was quiet. Too quiet. I gave them a gallon of milk and took some pitas out of the fridge. I pretended that everything was fine, but my trembling hands couldn't lie.

When the house became quiet, Samir and Seka walked on their tiptoes from our room, through the hallway, and down to the garage. I locked our room and followed them. When we reached the yard, I turned and looked at the building that was our home. The lights were on in different rooms, but their glow no longer seemed to have the warmth of home. I was so tired and cold. As we walked to Habiba's home, I shivered.

Habiba had made a comfortable bed for me, but I couldn't close my eyes with my mind racing with thoughts about our upcoming journey.

The Birth Certificate

My dear friend Yelena promised to give me her ID card so I could travel to Serbia. I thought, *It is true—that real friends are like a four-leaf clover: hard to find, lucky to have.* I needed a birth certificate for my son Samir, one with a Serbian name. Milan Rozic, one of Samir's school friends, lived in our neighborhood. I decided to go to Milan's home and ask his mother for a favor, but I realized full well that if she granted my request she would be putting herself in danger. After a sleepless night, with the first rooster calls I finally decided to go to the government office and ask for Milan's birth certificate without his or his parents' knowledge.

I arrived at the office feeling very nervous as if I were walking into a bank to rob it. When I recognized a former student, Maria, working there, I felt better.

"Hi, Mrs. Softic," she greeted me politely. "How can I help you?"

"I need a copy of my neighbor, Milan Rozic's, birth certificate. His mom asked me to do her a favor and get a copy of it for her while I was in town." It was a lie, of course.

"Do you know the date of his birth?" She looked at my hands, and I squeezed them to keep them from trembling. But my hands betrayed my true state of mind and kept shaking, so I put them into my pockets.

"Yes, yes. Milan was born on September 26, 1979, six months after my son." When I mentioned my son, Maria became quiet for a while, as if she had discovered my intention.

"Why didn't Mrs. Rozic come for the certificate herself?" She now looked at me suspiciously. A tinge of fire spread across my face, and I hid my eyes like a child caught stealing a cookie.

"And why does she need it?" Maria's body language and facial expression signaled that she was uncomfortable.

"I don't know. I didn't ask her," I blurted.

"Do you want to call and ask her?" Maria pushed the telephone towards me.

217

Oh my God, what should I do now? I thought. "Oh no, that's okay. She is working now, and I don't know her work number." I looked at the floor.

"Where does she work? I can find the number in the telephone book," Maria informed me. She walked towards the shelf. "Besides, her sister works in this building."

Another pang of fear stabbed my soul. *This wasn't as easy as I had imagined it would be.* "I don't want to disturb her at work." I paused. "If it's really a problem to get it now, I can tell Mrs. Rozic to come by another day." I sat making myself smaller, wanting to disappear from the room and from the world where my son and I could not travel as Muslims.

Maria was quiet for a moment. The seconds ticked by like hours, and finally I turned and grabbed the doorknob.

"Come here, Mrs. Softic."

I turned my head.

"You are my dear high school teacher and my principal. I like and respect you because you emphasized the importance of good character, and you were always ready to help your students. I still remember your sentence: 'Do good deeds, and do not regret doing them.'"

She removed a huge book from the shelf and sifted through the pages until she got to Milan's name. The hope of getting the document was slowly returning to my heart. I blinked several times in thankfulness that I had become a teacher, and that I had helped my students to build strong characters, stronger than the stupid rules of war.

"Mrs. Softic, please sit and relax for a moment. I'll get it ready for you now."

"I don't want to cause any problems for you." My mouth was tight and bitter as I forced the words out. She moved swiftly, her eyes glittered, and her fingers played on the keyboard like a skilled musician playing the piano. I sat on a chair and looked at the brave young lady who was putting her own job at risk to help me. She knew. It was clear enough that she had the courage when she saw an unjust rule to break it.

After about five minutes Maria gave me the birth certificate, and I saw the same brightness in her eyes that I saw on her graduation day when I handed her the diploma she had earned. I sighed. I couldn't say, "Thank you," to her, but my tears could.

Escape

On Saturday morning, we left from our new refuge, Habiba's house, before dawn and returned home. Dervisha followed me, quiet as an early morning breeze. Her tired eyes told me that she had had a sleepless night.

"The couple from Belgrade, Branko and Dara, came to my home last night," Dervisha told me. "They are returning to Belgrade tomorrow morning, so you and Samir need to be ready. Pack your suitcases, and when no one is paying attention, hide them in the garage. Be extremely careful on this trip."

"I can't just disappear from here without saying goodbye to my friends," I protested.

"You have to be smart and think of the journey ahead," urged Dervisha as we entered my room. "What would happen if the people in the house or your next door neighbor discover your plan? Do you remember what happened to Mina and Nijaz when they left their home? Your risk is many times worse." Dervisha dried her sweaty forehead as she spoke. "You are forty-five years old, but you behave like a child, and I am beginning to think that you will never mature."

"I think that I never was a child," I replied. "I watched our father die of a heart attack when I was only five. While the other kids played under our oak tree, I pulled weeds from the cornfield and measured how much milk our cows produced." I became quiet for a moment. "At age six I took care of my three-year-old brother, Alija. I wanted to be a good girl because I was terrified that our mother could die. She was our anchor, our protection, and our shield from storms, and I did not know how we would survive if she died." That old memory bubbled up like clear spring water from a hillside.

"One day my brother and I broke the window," I continued. "Mother came home exhausted, but she immediately noticed the missing windowpane. My heart was pounding, but I managed not to blink as she walked across the room to where I was standing. But rather than punish me as I feared, she encircled me with her arms, embracing me tightly, and told me in a gentle voice that one day everything would be fine."

Dervisha hugged me as my mother had when I was a child,

220

and our sobs filled the room.

"I am afraid now," I confided, "afraid that we will not make it across the border. I have already tried twice and failed both times."

"I have the feeling that you will make it this time," Dervisha replied, drying her eyes. "Believe me, I have a good feeling, but please be extremely careful."

As Dervisha left, I took my newest brown purse and walked to Yelena's house. The walk was one of ecstasy and agony. My mind first presented me with the image of Samir and myself successfully crossing the border and walking hand in hand on the far side of the Drina River. But that joyous picture lasted only long enough to make its dark twin that much more terrible. In the second image we were caught at the border, the police roughly pulling both of us from the car and throwing us in jail; our dream gone and our lives in peril.

"Oh dear God," I prayed under my breath, "Protect us on our trip!"

Yelena opened the door. Her eyes were tired and worried, the lines of strain on her forehead were deep, and there were strands of gray in her hair that I had not noticed before.

The words that were on the tip of my tongue rushed out. "We decided to leave—Sunday morning. Do you still feel like giving me your ID card?"

"Oh Aisa, yes! If I were able to share even my soul with you, I would do it this instant." Her eyes filled with tears, and we embraced. She walked to her bedroom and came back holding the ID card. Our arms brought us together in a second bittersweet embrace, and even the walls of the room seemed to cry with us.

"I don't know how to thank you," I voiced. "God will reward you for your courage and generous spirit. Please keep this brown purse as a remembrance of this moment." I paused. "If I get into any trouble, I will lie that I stole your ID card from this brown purse. Remember it."

"I hope you'll be fine. I don't want to think about anything else."

We walked together to the end of Yelena's street where we finally hugged each other one last time. I began to walk quickly away, but after about fifty meters I heard Yelena's voice again, "Aisa, wait!" She was almost running toward me, and my stomach immediately knotted. *Has she changed her mind? Does she want her ID card back?*

"I want to walk with you a little farther," she declared when she had caught up with me. "I don't know when or where we will have a chance to walk together again."

"Thank you, dear Yelena, but I think I'm under surveillance these days. I don't want to create any problems for you."

"I don't care." She put her vest across her shoulders. "Many people look at war as an opportunity to become rich. They bring back trucks, cars, furniture, and even clothes, things they looted from the people they fought against. I don't know why they would need all of those things. Greed I suppose." She paused. "The way you fought and survived here was an incredible feat of courage. Something inside me says that you will cross the border without any difficulty."

"I certainly hope so," I remarked softly. "My richness is the good people around me, especially you, my dear friend. I am thankful to God that He sent you to offer me your ID card. Without your help this trip would be impossible. Thank you for your enormous help. I admire you."

"No goodbyes today," Yelena replied. "I hope that we will see each other again someday." Yelena turned and walked fast to her home. I didn't look back. I only listened to her quick steps until they completely mixed with the faint sound of the spring breeze.

As I entered my house, I heard the sound of people's voices and the clink of coffee cups on saucers coming from the kitchen. I went immediately to my room focused on what Samir and I should pack. We would need summer clothes for now, but we had to travel light and would have to worry about winter clothes when the time came. Even so, for memory's sake I put the wool socks Mother had knitted for me and the children into the suitcase. When I opened the family picture album, the tears poured. I placed the album in my purse next to our documents.

Around sunset I walked to Mehmed's house. I sat in the same place where I had sat three years earlier when Husein and I had made the hard decision to separate for a time. I swallowed hard before I spoke, "It is no longer safe for Samir and me to stay in our home, and we will be leaving in the morning." I dried my eyes. "God knows that I did what was in my power, but for whatever reason it was not His will that I should succeed." I cleared my throat.

Mehmed, sighing, confessed how many times he had checked our home in the late hours of the night, worried about Samir and me. I thanked him and his wife, tearfully telling them that they had been like parents to me.

I prayed a long prayer at Habiba's house, asking God to protect us on our trip and to reward all those people who had helped us during these last few, very trying years. It was probably about midnight when the children finally fell asleep. The house was finally quiet, and it was the perfect moment to shed light on my plan.

"I have a secret to share with you," I whispered. "Samir and I are leaving tomorrow morning, *inshallah*." I swallowed hard, and my voice became shaky. "Please, keep us in your prayers. We plan to go to Belgrade."

"It is impossible." Habiba looked at me with eyes wide open. "Go to Belgrade, again? Why are you doing it? You couldn't pass the border a few months ago!"

I looked at them, half in fear, and half with courage. "You're right. It is risky, but I have no choice. It is too dangerous for Samir and me to remain in our home. I simply must put thoughts of what might go wrong at the border out of my mind. This time I have my friend's ID card."

"You'll be fine this time," encouraged Seka with a hint of a smile. "You have no other choice. Your husband and daughter await you in the United States. God knows your courage and your love for your family."

"I deeply appreciate your help. Thank you from the bottom of my heart," I declared softly.

Habiba supported her chin with her hand, sighing. "You helped us too. You taught me to pray. Even though the war is all around us, I feel the deepest peace I have ever felt. I had the best Ramadan of my life since I have learned how important it is to build closeness to God." She became silent for a few seconds. "I will try to join my brother and sister in Sweden."

Seka looked through the window into the distance, lamenting, "We don't have anybody to sponsor us. I don't know how we are going to survive."

"I'll try to bring you to the United States once I am there," I promised, touching her hand.

With the first trace of dawn I awoke from an easy sleep. Reassuring images from my dream raced through my head, and I thanked God for the good sign. In my dream I was driving a car. I slowed down as I approached the point where the street became one-way in the opposite direction I was traveling. Looking from the sign, I noticed that the street in front of me was empty. I considered my options for a moment and then carefully continued, even though I was driving against the one-way signs. The end of the one-way street connected me to traffic in both directions. As I merged into normal traffic, I woke up.

A hard rain beat against Habiba's window. I performed the *fajr* prayer, the prayer before sunrise, while Habiba made coffee.

"We don't know when we will drink coffee together again," I remarked with a touch of bitterness in my voice. "It is very hard to leave you, and I will never forget you." Habiba quietly cried, her face buried in her hands. Samir, who had just awakened, walked slowly through the room and opened the door. Seka and I went outside where the morning rain washed away our tears.

A white car approached the house. My sister signaled for me to open the garage door, and the car slid slowly in.

Petar, a middle-aged gentleman, about my height, confused me with his first words. "Could we postpone our trip until next weekend? This is a very dangerous journey we are embarking on, you know."

I searched for Dervisha's eyes, but she looked at Petar. "I don't see any reason for changing the plan. This trip will always be dangerous."

"Let me see your friend's ID card," stated Dara, Petar's wife. She look at the card carefully, raised her eyes and looked at my face. "I hope we'll be fine. They have some similarities, but if someone looks carefully, differences are noticeable." Dara looked at the card again.

"Dervisha is right. This trip will be always dangerous," agreed Petar. He moved closer to me and whispered, "I want to help you, but what happens if we have problems at the border?"

"We have problems here already. We can't even sleep in our home." I looked at Samir. "If we face problems on our way, I will not blame you. You have come to help Samir and me, and I will never be able to thank you enough."

Petar looked through the garage window. "I am building a weekend home. That lumber you have behind the garage would make a good roof. Could Zaim, Dervisha's son, come with my friend and take it?"

"Of course," Dervisha and I agreed, almost in unison.

"Come Samir. Let's get the suitcases in the trunk," urged Petar.

I tiptoed quietly to the room, dressed, and took one last look. Nana's shoes grabbed my attention. I put them on my chest and hugged them tightly to me. Their warmth filled my soul. I left the shoes in their place with several marks of my tears on them and returned to the garage. Petar and Dara were already in the front seat of the car. Dervisha opened the back door, and Samir and I squeezed in.

This is my sister Dervisha, my big supporter.

The Other Side of the River

Slowly the car moved toward the street. Our dog looked at us. The bowl of food we had set out the night before sat untouched in front of her. I could not risk one last look at her for fear she would bark and awaken the people in our house and in the neighborhood. I sat back, listening to the rain pounding the car, and watched the neighborhood as it slid by. I closed my eyes, and the memories of two decades of our life in this neighborhood occupied my mind. Tears showered my face, and it looked like the whole neighborhood was crying with me.

As we entered Dubrave, Dervisha squeezed my hand and gave Samir a love tap on his shoulder. "Good luck my dear sister and my nephew."

The car stopped. My sister got out and didn't look back. She walked away from the car, and I imagined walking back with her to my childhood. Now I had not only cut all ties with those I had known and loved, but also, temporarily would deny even my name. My heart cried.

Dara turned her head toward me and disclosed, "We are all losers in this terrible war. Petar and I worked hard in Germany and built a weekend house on the Adriatic seashore in Croatia, but now, as Serbs, we cannot go there."

Suddenly the car stopped. A Serb soldier came up to the car. Dara gave him her front seat and squeezed into the back with Samir and me. I froze in fear.

Why on earth did Petar pick up that soldier? Did he want to help him, or did he think the soldier could help us somehow? Wasn't Petar afraid of an unexpected police or military patrol?

As we traveled through one destroyed village after another, the soldier talked about the battles he had been in. He smiled when he told us how soldiers from Serbia had come to help them to "free" those villages. "Muslims and Croats fought together; but when we captured several Muslims, we asked the Croats to free them. The Croats told us to do whatever we wanted to do with them." Petar and the soldier laughed. "Muslims certainly paid the highest price in this war," the soldier continued. "Both of us, we Serbs and the Croats, have our countries behind us. They support us like a mother would support her children. But what do the Muslims have?"

I could barely hold back my tears and anger as I listened to the soldier ramble on.

The soldier got out of the car at the edge of Brcko, and a cold, tense atmosphere took his place. Petar lit a cigarette, and the smoke so nauseated me that I had to open the window for fresh air. I recognized the house where we had stopped when I traveled in December. I felt a stabbing pain in my stomach again. My hands became ice-cold, so I closed the window.

We are so close to the border. What is waiting for us there? What if they recognize me? And if the policemen realize that I'm not the same person whose picture is on the ID card, will they arrest me? What would they do with Samir? He has to know everything on that document. Oh dear God help us.

I opened my purse and took out the false birth certificate. "Samir," I whispered, "you are Milan Rozic. Your birthday is September 26. The year and place are as your own. Your mother is Nada, and your father is Miroslav." I closed my eyes. "Memorize all the information." I had trouble keeping myself from throwing up as I simultaneously gave Samir his instructions and wrestled with the fear.

"Mom, what is wrong?" Samir asked. His face lost its natural color.

"I'm scared. I was here a few months ago and had a lot of trouble."

I cleared my throat and called to Dara, "If I have any trouble getting through, please take Samir to Belgrade with you. The birth

227

certificate does not have any connection with me." My mouth was dry, and it became harder and harder to pronounce words.

"I have another concern about your son," Dara added, "but I will ask you about it later."

"I'm frightened," confided Petar, lighting another cigarette. "We cannot go straight to the border." He took a handkerchief, dried his hands, and then tucked it in his shirt. Dara, leaning over from her seat, whispered something in his ear. Peter scratched his head and informed us, "We are going to visit our friends before we cross. My friend has a boat, and we may decide to use it to cross the Drina River after midnight. My friends are willing to help us."

The car stopped in front of a house in a quiet village neighborhood. Petar announced, "My wife, my friends, and I are going to make a final decision. You two stay in the car." He closed the door.

Dara looked at me and asked, "Can we talk outside for a moment?" She stood behind the car and whispered, "Is Samir circumcised?"

Her question astonished me. Circumcision is mandated by Islam. Muslim males are all circumcised.

"Yes. Why are you asking?" I paused. "Are they going to check it?" I froze.

"They could. I don't know," she answered and headed to the house.

I went back to the car, squeezed my eyes shut, and hunched my back, as though I could somehow hide from whatever might be coming. My head felt like it was coming apart, and my entire body was covered in sweat.

Samir looked at me. "Mom, are you okay? You don't look so good."

"I am not sure about this trip anymore. It's too dangerous," I whispered.

"Mom, we are almost there. In another half hour, if God will help us, we will be out of this war zone. We'll be fine." He patted my tense shoulder.

With a sigh I looked into my son's bright eyes. His hope touched my heart, calming me for the moment.

"You're right. I had a good dream a few nights ago. With God's help everything is possible." I paused. "Samir, let's pray."

Our lips moved as we recited our prayers. *Dear God, You conduct our entire universe. We are asking You by all of Your names to help us today to cross to the other side of the river safely. We want to go to a safe place and glorify Your name.*

"It's time to go." Petar seemed little more relaxed as he settled himself in the driver's seat.

I squeezed Samir's hand tightly, and he gave me a calm, confident look.

After a few minutes of driving, we slowed, almost coming to a stop. The hundreds of cars in front of us and surrounding us created a large knot in front of the border gates. Drums played so loudly in my ears that they muted any sounds from the outside world. I tried to speak, but bitterness glued my lips shut. We stopped. I dried my palms. *Was there an accident in front of us?* Suddenly I recognized the offices, the gates, and the place where I was thrown off the buses twice. Once again those agonizing memories became vivid, and I heard a voice in my mind saying, "I thought that our Republic had been cleaned out by now, but look, the Muslim is still here! How dare you come here! What do you want here?" My body felt numb.

The color drain out of Samir's face. I opened the car window to get air. I looked at my face in the rearview mirror and met Petar's eyes. He quickly put the car in gear, turned into an emergency lane, and drove straight to the border gates. When he squeezed the car back into line, Dara looked surprised that no one had stopped him.

Ah, the border. To be or not to be. The car in front of us was waved through. A border officer came up to Petar's car. I saw his dark blue uniform and black shoes, but I was afraid to raise my head. Fear paralyzed me. *What do I need to do with my eyes?* I looked at the car floor. *The officer would notice that my face and the photo on the card do not match.* I became sick, ready to vomit. With shaking hands I handed the ID card and the birth certificate to the officer. *I have to look at him. It will be less suspicious.* Our eyes met. Cold sweat glued my clothes to my body, and a hundred invisible nails pierced my flesh. I lowered my head until my chin touched my chest and closed my eyes. I tasted the bitterness in my dry mouth and heard only the music of dead drums in my ears. Time stopped. Seconds lasted forever.

Suddenly the sound of paperwork changing hands broke the silence. Petar put the car in gear, and we began to move forward. I raised my head, and at the same time the barrier was lifted and the car moved up onto the bridge. I almost strangled Samir with a bear hug. A brightness from his eyes melted my heart, and I wiped tears of happiness from my face. My muscles began lessening the grip they had held on every part of my body for so long in my life.

Dear God, this journey is Your reward. I tried to pass the border twice before and failed. Thank you for accompanying my son and me with good people who helped us to pass the border. Please reward all of them.

I rolled down the window, and thousands of suns smiled at me from the sparkling river. A stone in the river, the same color and the shape as Nana's shoes, caught my gaze. *The water, continuously moving down, shaped the stone. Sometimes with the gentle caress of summer, then with muddy ranging power in the fall, then the choking cold of winter ice and the violent rush of spring floods, the water taps the stone's top, squeezes its sides, and even forges its inside.. The river is the same, but the water comes new and different, flowing like our days. I might bring Nana's shoes and place the stone inside them. The shoes could shield the smooth stone's surface from bloody water, from salty tears, and from bullet shells. Inside the shoes, the stone could enjoy the soft sound of people respectful conversation who are crossing the bridge referring happily to each other by their true names.* I couldn't move my eyes from the stone until we passed the bridge. I turned my head back, looked at the Drina River and whispered, "Good-bye my dear stone! Good-by my dear country! Good-bye, my dear river! I will be far from you, but you'll be in my heart all my life!"

The Fall of 2010

In this telling of my life story I explained that on a day in December 1992, my principal in Bosnia made a joke about denying me a bonus. He laughed when he told me that the bonus was only for those teachers who celebrated Christmas, in other words, not for me because I was Muslim. "I will give you the special increase for your holiday, Eid, isn't it?" Of course the bonus never came, and I eventually lost my teaching position because of my Islamic faith. It had been a long and challenging road I had walked since that day in 1992 when I had been laughed out of my principal's office with an insult both to my faith and to my worthiness as a teacher.

Fast forward now to the fall of 2010. Here I was, an American citizen and once again a teacher, a respected member of the profession I loved. In addition, I now had a master's degree in education.

It was November 17, 2010, the date of my holiday Eid, one of the two holidays in Islam. That day was payday at my school. When I opened my pay envelope, I found that the raise I had earned with my master's degree was now a permanent part of my salary. I had to smile that the date for my "bonus" was perfectly set. It had taken eighteen years, but my "bonus" had finally come through! It had been a long, perilous walk indeed.

God does not share with us His plan for our lives, but if we live in faith, He will shower us with His blessings. From my journey I have come to understand God's words, "Be patient [in adversity], for, verily, God will not let the reward of the righteous be wasted."[3]

---

[3] *The Holy Qur'an*, Chapter 11, Verse 115.

Aisa and Samir reuniting with Husein and Aida in the United States at Dayton's airport 1995.

"Refugee No More," an article about Asia in City Beats *from 2006*

Alija (my brother), me, and Suada (his wife) in Sweden 2008.

About the Author

Aisa Softic is now an American citizen, proud to be a part of this country that has opened the gate of opportunity to her and her family. But a part of her heart will always be in Bosnia.

She has been living with her husband, Husein, in Cincinnati, Ohio for the last twenty years. Her true passion is teaching. After studying in Dayton, Ohio, she became a special education teacher in 2001. Asia is happy to teach students with special needs because she is able to relate to them and see how it is difficult to communicate when people around you are unable to understand you. Asia is also very active in the American-Bosnian community.

Made in United States
North Haven, CT
11 December 2021

12468419R00137